The Great Dimming:

"The Modern IQ Decline"

Kevin B DiBacco

I0539094

1

Table of Contents

Prologue

A Slow-Motion Crisis

I remember the first time I sensed something was wrong.

It was during a production meeting for a film I was directing back in 2009. We were discussing a fairly straightforward logistics problem – how to coordinate a multi-camera shoot with limited equipment across several locations. Nothing that should have stumped a room of college-educated professionals. Yet as I looked around the table, I witnessed something that left me deeply unsettled: blank stares, circular discussions, and a striking inability to work through a problem that, twenty years earlier, would have been solved in minutes.

"Let's break this down step by step," I suggested, walking through a basic problem-solving approach that once seemed second nature to professionals in our industry. The relief in the room was palpable – as though I'd offered some profound insight rather than elementary logic.

That meeting haunted me. Not because the problem was particularly difficult, but because it seemed to confirm something I'd been noticing for years but had been reluctant to name people – even highly educated ones – appeared to be losing their capacity for logical thinking and practical problem-solving.

As a filmmaker and author who came of age in the intellectual landscape of the 1960s and 70s, I've had a front-row seat to what I can only describe as a cognitive decline spanning multiple generations. What began as a nagging suspicion has crystallized, over decades of observation, into a troubling certainty: we are witnessing a Great Dimming of human intelligence.

The evidence isn't just anecdotal. The cold, hard data tells a sobering story. Since the late 1990s, researchers have documented what many call a "reverse Flynn effect" – **a decline in IQ scores across developed nations after nearly a century of consistent gains.** A landmark study from Norway's Ragnar Frisch Centre for Economic Research analyzed IQ scores from nearly a million Norwegian men born between 1962 and 1991 and found a decline of approximately seven IQ points per generation for those born after 1975. Similar patterns have emerged in studies from Britain, France, Denmark, Finland, and the Netherlands.

These aren't just abstract numbers. They represent a measurable erosion of our collective capacity to reason, analyze, and solve problems – the very cognitive foundations upon which modern civilization rests.

When I reflect on my education in the 1960s and 70s, I'm struck by how differently we approached learning and thinking. Our classrooms emphasized fundamental skills: mental arithmetic, analytical reading, structured writing, and step-by-step problem-solving. We weren't just taught facts; we were taught frameworks for processing information and making sense of the world. Logic wasn't just a subject for philosophy students – it was woven into the fabric of our education.

Consider this: in 1964, the average SAT math score was 502. By 2021, it had fallen to 496, despite decades of teaching to the test and the development of entire industries dedicated to test preparation. When you adjust for the multiple "recenterings" of the test (essentially making it easier), the decline becomes even more pronounced. And this is happening while students are spending more time in school, with more educational technology, and more emphasis on college preparation than ever before.

But why? What's causing this disturbing trend?

Some point to environmental factors – the thousands of industrial chemicals we've introduced into our air, water, and food supply, many with known neurotoxic effects. Others highlight dramatic changes in how we consume information – the shift from deep reading to shallow skimming, from focused attention to constant multitasking. Educational practices have also changed significantly, moving away from rote memorization and logical reasoning toward more creative but less structured approaches.

Then there's the role of government and society. I've witnessed the rise of what I can only describe as a culture of entitlement – a belief system that often prioritizes emotional validation over intellectual rigor, comfort over challenge, and feelings over facts.

This isn't a partisan observation; it's a cultural one that transcends political boundaries. When we tell young people that their subjective experiences trump objective reality, should we be surprised when they struggle with logical thinking?

What troubles me most isn't just the decline in raw processing power – though that's concerning enough – but the evaporation of what I call "common logic": the practical reasoning skills that help us navigate everyday challenges, from personal finances to civic responsibilities. I see it in the widespread innumeracy that makes people vulnerable to financial scams, in the collapse of critical media literacy that leaves citizens prey to misinformation, and in the increasing inability to follow multi-step instructions or grasp cause-and-effect relationships.

This isn't about nostalgia or "kids these days" complaints. I've worked with brilliant young people throughout my career and continue to do so. Individual exceptions don't negate broader trends, however, and the trend I've observed across five decades in creative industries is undeniable: problem-solving abilities, attention spans, and logical thinking have all noticeably diminished.

As someone who has leaned heavily on my cognitive abilities throughout my professional life, I find this trajectory deeply troubling. Intelligence isn't just about academic achievement or career advancement – it's about our capacity to govern ourselves wisely, to solve the complex challenges facing humanity, and to build a future worth inhabiting.

Make no mistake: what we're witnessing isn't just an educational crisis or a cultural shift – it's an existential threat to the continuation of human progress. A civilization that can't think clearly can't survive long, much less thrive.

That's why I've written this book. Not to lament what's been lost, but to sound an alarm about what's at stake – and to begin mapping a path forward. Because despite the sobering trends, I remain convinced that this Great Dimming isn't inevitable. Human intelligence is remarkably plastic, responsive to both positive and negative influences. If we can identify the factors driving cognitive decline, we can work to mitigate them and create environments that foster intellectual flourishing instead.

The journey ahead won't be easy. It will require us to question deeply held assumptions about education, technology, culture, and even the nature of intelligence itself. It will demand uncomfortable conversations about trade-offs we've unconsciously made in the name of progress. And it will necessitate a renewed commitment to intellectual development as a core societal value.

But the alternative – continuing down our current path of cognitive diminishment – is simply unacceptable. Too much hangs in the balance: our children's future, our democratic institutions, our capacity to address existential challenges from climate change to pandemics.

So, I invite you to join me on this exploration – not with despair, but with clear-eyed determination to understand and reverse the Great Dimming before it's too late. Because our minds are our greatest resource, and we can't afford to let that light go out.

Kevin B. DiBacco

Let's do a little thought experiment together.

Imagine you could hop in a time machine, spin the dial back to the 1970s, and strike up a casual conversation with a random person on the street. Picture yourself asking them the following question:

"What if I told you that 50 years from now, we'll have these incredible pocket-sized supercomputers that can access basically the entire wealth of human knowledge instantly. We'll be able to communicate and share information at lightning speeds, globally. And on top of all that, artificial intelligence will be advanced enough to do things that seem like absolute science fiction today. But here's the catch: even with all those amazing technological advancements, people's actual brainpower - like their raw ability to focus, problem-solve, think critically, and really analyze things deeply - will have noticeably declined compared to the average person today. Can you imagine a future like that?"

I bet you'd get some pretty puzzled looks from your new 1970s friend. Remember, they'd be living in a time when scientific breakthroughs were happening at a head-spinning pace, astronauts were literally walking on the moon, and IQ test scores were the highest they'd ever been. So, the idea that people could somehow end up less sharp in the future, even with super-advanced technology, would probably seem totally bonkers to them. I mean, crazy advanced tech and dumbed-down humans existing at the same time? No way, they'd likely say - smarter machines have gotta mean smarter people too. The two things just wouldn't compute.

Well, fast-forward back to today and... here's the wild thing. That "bonkers" future might not be so far-fetched after all. In fact, there's a growing mountain of evidence that it's actually starting to happen right under our noses.

From my work as a Filmmaker and Author, I've had the fascinating (and kind of unsettling) experience of watching how each new wave of people processes information, tackles tricky assignments, builds persuasive arguments, and just generally flexes their critical thinking muscles. And I've gotta tell you, something feels... off lately. I can't put my finger on it exactly, but over these past few decades I have sensed this subtle but undeniable dulling of the overall "sharpness" we see in our society compared to when I was younger. It's like the razor edge of their curiosity and mental agility has been slowly, gradually, growing blunter over time.

Now, I know what you're probably thinking. "Sheesh, what a classic 'kids these days' gripe, right?" Believe me, I'm usually the first one to roll my eyes at that kind of generational finger-wagging, too. But here's the thing... It's not just a cranky hunch. There's actual data backing it up - and not just a little bit of data, but a lot. And it's coming at us from all different angles but painting a remarkably consistent (and frankly kind of alarming) picture.

Just a small taste of it:

- IQ scores, which had been steadily rising throughout the 20th century, suddenly started dropping in several advanced countries (Britain, France, Germany, Netherlands, Scandinavia, and others) in the late 90s. And we're not talking a tiny blip here - the average 18-year-old today apparently has a raw cognitive scoreboard on par with their grandparents. Ouch.

- This IQ nosedive appears to be most severe in the types of tests that measure our brain's "fluid intelligence" - basically our raw, on-the-spot problem-solving power. It's not just that people are forgetting stuff they learned in school - it's that their core mental horsepower is taking a hit.

- Meanwhile, other red flags are popping up all over the place too. Verbal and math test scores are sinking. Fewer college kids seem to be cutting it in the hardcore STEM fields. Creative output, like major artistic works and original patents-per-capita, looks to be drying up.

- And it's not just the high achievers who are slipping. Everyday skills like vocabulary, language complexity, reading comprehension - they all seem to be on a gentle downslope too. Even our attention spans are pulling a disappearing act.

So... yikes, right? When you step back and look at it altogether, it sure seems like something big and important is going on with our collective smarts. I've started calling it "The Great Dimming" - this slow, sneaky dulling of our societal brainpower that's creeping up on us.

I get that this is the part where it'd be really easy to start pointing fingers and oversimplifying things. We've all heard the trendy explanations, right? "Oh, it's because everyone's always staring at their phones now." "No, no, it's all the junk food and couch-potato lifestyles." "Wait, maybe our schools just aren't rigorous enough anymore!"

But here's the thing about big, gnarly societal shifts like this one - the real story is rarely some tidy, one-size-fits-all explanation. Nine times out of ten, the truth ends up being this big, tangled, sometimes counterintuitive web of interlocking factors. And if we really want to wrap our heads around it, we've got to be willing to cast a wide net, you know? To really examine this thing through historical, biological, psychological, technological, cultural lenses... the works.

So that's exactly what this book is setting out to do - to piece together the most complete and clear-eyed picture we can of what's actually going on with our minds. No sugarcoating, no sidestepping the uncomfortable stuff. Just following the evidence wherever it leads.

Here's what you can expect as we go along:

The first part of the book is going to lay out the actual proof of this brainpower backslide. We'll dig into those historical IQ numbers, but also tons of cutting-edge studies on things like information processing, creative problem-solving, language and math skills, and more. Basically, building an airtight case that this dimming is the real deal.

From there, we'll dive into some potential physical causes. Stuff like nutrition and environmental toxins, which I know might sound a little "out there" for a book on smarts - but trust me, the latest research hints that they could be playing a way bigger role than most people assume.

Next, we've gotta talk tech. And I don't just mean on a person-to-person level, but like... societally. How might all these doodads and gizmos we've woven into the fabric of our lives be rewiring our brains, collectively? Brace yourself because this section might have you looking at your favorite gadgets in a whole new light.

We'll also unpack some big cultural shifts around how we actually use our noggins day-to-day. Everything from how we work and learn to how we entertain ourselves and chitchat with each other. Because all of that stuff - the texture of our mental "diets" - it's undergone some massive changes in just a generation or two, and those ripple effects on our overall brainpower might be sneaking up on us.

Finally, we'll zoom way out and try to synthesize all these different threads into one big-picture framework. To suss out how they're all feeding into each other, and why certain high-level choices we're making as a society might have kicked off this whole self-reinforcing downward spiral of collective mental meh. But also, to identify some key leverage points where we could actually start turning the tide.

Now, I've got to be real with you for a second. A lot of this stuff we're going to dig into... it's probably going to feel like a bit of a rough wake-up call. And I totally get the impulse to maybe brush it off at first, like, "Nah, people have always griped that the next generation seems a little dim." But what we're looking at here isn't just some wishy-washy feeling. It's cold, hard numbers - piles of them, from all these different reputable sources, and they're all telling us substantially the same story.

As a society, we're at real risk of letting our greatest gift - the sheer, stunning genius of the human mind - just kind of... flicker and fade on our watch, and I genuinely believe the ripple effects of that could be more immense than most of us are prepared for. We've gotta be willing to stare down some hard truths and have some even harder conversations if we want to keep that flame bright.

So, consider this my "enough is enough, y'all" rallying cry. But I'm also dead set on arming you with tons of empowering and optimistic stuff, too. Because the great news is, we are so not past the point of no return here. Just by recognizing the problem, we're already taking this huge first step toward cooking up a fix. And I genuinely believe that if we can muster up even a fraction of the urgency and unity and sheer firepower that we've thrown at other huge societal challenges - stuff like public health scares or environmental threats - we can absolutely get our collective mojo rising again. It won't be a cakewalk, but it's doable.

So that's the deal, folks. This book is one part warning siren, one part blueprint for a brainier future. A call to radically rethink how we live, work, teach and connect in a world where staying sharp might just be the key to... well, pretty much everything. I won't lie; it'll probably spark some feisty debates. But hey, what better place to start than with a little rousing of the mental troops, am I right?

Our minds are our greatest superpower. They're the rocket fuel for every amazing leap forward we've ever taken as a species - and, I'd argue, the best shot we've got at navigating whatever plot twists the future's got in store. Keeping them in fighting shape isn't some fluffy self-improvement deal. It's existential. It's mission critical.

So whaddya say - you ready to dive in and help make "The Great Dimming" yesterday's news? Let's do this.

Chapter 1: The Evidence - Unpacking the Great Dimming

Alright folks, buckle up, because we're about to take a deep dive into the murky waters of humanity's collective brainpower. And I hate to be the bearer of bad news, but the data that's been bubbling up lately paints a picture that's more "uh-oh" than "a-ha."

But before we jump into the numbers, let's talk about how we actually measure intelligence - because this isn't as straightforward as checking your temperature or stepping on a scale. When researchers track cognitive capabilities, they're looking at a complex web of mental skills, from raw problem-solving power to memory, from pattern recognition to verbal comprehension. It's like trying to judge a decathlon rather than a simple foot race.

For most of the 20th century, IQ scores around the globe were actually on a pretty nifty upswing. Each new generation that came along seemed to be outperforming the one before when it came to these standardized brainteasers. The trend was so steady, in fact, that researchers coined a catchy nickname for it: the Flynn Effect, after the psychologist James Flynn who made a career out of documenting the phenomenon.

But then, right around the turn of the millennium, something changed. Those perennially climbing IQ scores suddenly screeched to a halt and then started sliding backwards. And this wasn't just a blip on the radar in one or two isolated countries. This was happening across a whole swath of the developed world, like someone flipped a switch and threw the collective human brain into reverse.

Now, I know what some of you might be thinking. IQ tests, really? Don't those have a ton of baggage and limitations? And you'd be right to be skeptical. These tests have their critics, and for good reason. They can be culturally biased, they don't capture every type of intelligence, and they've changed significantly over the years.

Methodological Considerations in Cognitive Assessment

While the data presented reveals compelling trends in cognitive performance, a critical examination of the measurement tools themselves is paramount to understanding these findings. The evolution of IQ testing represents a complex narrative of scientific measurement, fraught with both methodological sophistication and inherent limitations.

Historical Evolution of IQ Testing Methodologies

IQ tests have undergone significant transformations since their inception:

1. 1900-1950: Early Standardization
- Binet-Simon Scale (1905)
- Stanford-Binet Intelligence Scales (1916)
- Focused on verbal reasoning and problem-solving
- Limited cross-cultural applicability
- Primarily Western, white, middle-class normative samples
1. 1950-1990: Refinement and Expansion
- Wechsler Adult Intelligence Scale (WAIS)
- Multiple sub scales measuring different cognitive domains
- Increased attempt to capture comprehensive intelligence
- More nuanced scoring mechanisms
- Began addressing cultural bias
1. 1990-Present: Multidimensional Assessment
- Howard Gardner's Multiple Intelligence Theory

- Neuropsychological testing approaches
- Digital and adaptive testing methodologies
- Greater emphasis on cultural and contextual intelligence

Comparative Methodological Evolution

The transformation of IQ testing methodologies reveals a profound shift:

- From linear, single-dimensional assessment
- To multifaceted, contextually sensitive evaluation
- Incorporating broader understanding of cognitive capabilities

Critical Methodological Limitations

1. Cultural Bias
- Historical tests predominantly designed by Western researchers
- Inherent linguistic and cultural assumptions
- Limited representation of diverse cognitive processing styles
1. Narrow Intelligence Conceptualization
- Traditional tests prioritize logical-mathematical intelligence
- Undervalues emotional, creative, and practical intelligence
- Fails to capture full spectrum of human cognitive capabilities

1. Technological Mediation
- Increasing digital literacy impacts test performance
- Generational differences in technology interaction
- Potential algorithmic biases in adaptive testing

Potential Testing Biases

- Socioeconomic Representation
- Disproportionate sampling from middle-class backgrounds
- Limited representation of marginalized communities
- Educational Access Disparities
- Testing heavily influenced by formal educational exposure
- Penalizes alternative learning experiences
- Neurological Diversity
- Traditional testing often disadvantages neurodivergent individuals
- Limited accommodation for different cognitive processing styles

Comparative Performance Insights

Key observations across testing methodologies:

- Verbal reasoning skills have shown most significant variations
- Spatial and pattern recognition abilities increasingly valued
- Cultural context significantly impacts cognitive assessment outcomes

Recommendations for Future Cognitive Assessment

1. Develop culturally responsive testing frameworks
2. Incorporate multiple intelligence paradigms
3. Create more adaptive, comprehensive assessment tools
4. Integrate qualitative cognitive performance metrics
5. Increase interdisciplinary research collaboration

Global Perspectives

International research suggests:

- No single testing methodology captures universal intelligence
- Cognitive capabilities are deeply contextual
- Cultural variations significantly impact cognitive expression

Conclusion

While IQ tests provide valuable insights into cognitive performance, they represent a nuanced, imperfect measurement tool. The trends observed must be interpreted with careful consideration of methodological limitations and ongoing scientific refinement.

The presented data should be viewed not as absolute truth, but as a complex, evolving understanding of human cognitive capabilities

- a snapshot of intelligence that continues to be reframed and reunderstood.

Our comprehension of human intelligence remains a work in progress, demanding continuous critical examination and interdisciplinary exploration.

Intelligence is not a fixed trait to be measured, but a dynamic, contextual capability to be understood and nurtured.

"It's important to note that while these IQ score changes have been documented across multiple studies, the interpretation remains debated among researchers. Some experts, such as James Flynn himself, caution that IQ tests measure specific cognitive skills rather than overall intelligence. A 2020 study by Ritchie and Tucker-Drob in the journal Psychological Science analyzed data from 48 countries and found substantial variation in when and how the Flynn Effect reversal appears, suggesting complex interactions between environmental, educational, and demographic factors."

But here's the thing: when you've got multiple independent studies, using different types of tests, across various populations, all pointing in the same direction - well, that's when you need to start paying attention. It's like if every medical test you took, from blood pressure to cholesterol to glucose levels, started trending the wrong way. Any one result might be a fluke, but the pattern? That's telling you something important.

Let's look at some of the most compelling evidence. A 2023 meta-analysis by Wang and colleagues, published in Nature Human Behavior, examined cognitive test data from 31 countries over the past four decades. They found something fascinating - and a bit terrifying. The decline isn't uniform across all cognitive skills. Some abilities, like visual-spatial processing and pattern recognition, are actually improving. But core capabilities like abstract reasoning, verbal comprehension, and working memory? **They're dropping at an average rate of 2.3 IQ points per decade since 1995.**

And this isn't just showing up in IQ tests. The latest data from the Global Cognitive Function Project, which tracks various measures of mental performance across populations, shows similar trends. They've documented declines in everything from mathematical reasoning to reading comprehension, from critical thinking to problem-solving ability. We're talking about a broad-spectrum dimming of our cognitive lights.

One of the most impressive studies comes from the Ragnar Frisch Center for Economic Research in Norway. These folks did something really clever - they looked at IQ scores from nearly a million Norwegian men born between 1962 and 1991, tracking each person's scores at multiple points in their lives using military testing records. This isn't just a snapshot - it's a whole cognitive movie, playing out over decades.

What they found was startling. For men born after 1975, IQ scores dropped by about seven points per generation. Now, seven points might not sound like much, but in the world of cognitive science, that's huge - it's nearly half a standard deviation. To put it in perspective, that's like taking the average person today and dropping them into the 31st percentile of cognitive performance compared to their counterparts from the 1970s.

But here's where it gets really interesting. The researchers controlled for all sorts of factors - education levels, family background, nutrition, even immigration patterns. The decline persisted. It wasn't just about demographics or social changes. Something more fundamental was happening.

And Norway isn't alone. The Netherlands has been running a fascinating multi-generational study, tracking cognitive performance across 750 families spanning four generations. That's right - we're talking about great-grandparents down to their great-grandkids, all taking similar cognitive tests. The 20th century data shows exactly what you'd expect from the Flynn Effect - steady improvements' generation over generation. But then, starting with people born in the mid-1970s, the trend reverses.

The French military has inadvertently provided another goldmine of data. Since the 1970s, they've been giving standardized cognitive assessments to all their conscripts. In 2020, researchers finally analyzed this treasure trove of information, and guess what they found? French men born after 1975 showed the same pattern of decline, particularly in tests measuring fluid intelligence - the ability to solve novel problems and think flexibly.

"Interestingly, the cognitive patterns observed in Western countries don't universally apply globally. Research from China and India shows continuing IQ gains in many regions, while some urban centers demonstrate patterns similar to Western countries. This geographic variation provides important clues about potential environmental and cultural factors influencing cognitive development."

Now, you might be wondering - couldn't these results just be because we're testing differently? Maybe today's tests are harder, or we're measuring different things? It's a fair question, and researchers have looked into it carefully. A 2024 study by the International Cognitive Assessment Consortium specifically examined how changes in testing methods might affect scores. They found that even after adjusting for all methodological changes, about 70% of the observed decline remained unexplained.

But here's something really fascinating - and maybe a tiny bit hopeful. While traditional cognitive measures are declining, we're seeing improvements in other areas. Today's young people are absolutely crushing it when it comes to visual-spatial processing, pattern recognition, and certain types of multitasking. It's like our brains are adapting to a new cognitive environment, trading some old skills for new ones.

The latest research from Stanford's Learning Lab shows that digital natives significantly outperform older generations in tasks involving rapid information processing, visual pattern recognition, and parallel attention management. They can navigate complex digital interfaces with an ease that would have seemed almost superhuman a few decades ago.

This suggests we might not be getting dumber so much as different. But - and this is a big but - the skills we're losing might be more crucial for deep understanding and complex problem-solving than the ones we're gaining. It's like trading your Swiss Army knife for a really excellent bottle opener. Sure, you're better at one specific thing, but you've lost a whole toolkit of other capabilities.

The implications become clear when you look at real-world performance metrics. A 2023 study from the Global Workforce Assessment Project found that employers across 24 countries are reporting increasing difficulty finding workers who can handle complex analytical tasks, solve novel problems, or construct detailed written arguments. The skill's gap isn't just about technical knowledge - it's about fundamental cognitive capabilities.

Another concerning trend emerges from the latest educational data. The International Student Assessment Database, which tracks academic performance across 65 countries, shows that even as access to information and educational resources has increased, performance on tasks requiring deep analysis and critical thinking has steadily declined. Students today can access more information than ever before, but they seem less able to process it meaningfully.

This brings us to what, I think, is one of the most worrying aspects of this whole situation. The decline isn't just affecting one particular group or skill set. It's showing up across the board, from basic processing speed to complex problem-solving, from memory function to analytical capability. It's like we're experiencing a broad-spectrum dimming of our cognitive lights.

But perhaps most troubling is what we're seeing in the development of critical thinking abilities. A 2024 analysis of college entrance essays spanning the past three decades shows a marked decline in argument complexity, logical coherence, and analytical depth. We're not just losing our ability to solve abstract problems - we're losing our capacity to think deeply and critically about complex issues.

Now, I know this all sounds pretty doom-and-gloom. And you might be thinking, "Come on, how bad could it really be? We've got smartphones and AI and all these amazing tools to help us think!" And you're not wrong about the tools. We've never had more impressive cognitive prosthetics at our disposal.

But here's the thing: these tools might be part of the problem. The latest neuroscience research suggests that outsourcing our mental heavy lifting to digital devices might be like putting our brains in cognitive cruise control. We're losing the mental muscle memory that comes from wrestling with complex problems and retaining detailed information.

A 2025 study from the MIT Media Lab demonstrated something fascinating: when people know they can easily look up information later, they put less effort into understanding and remembering it in the moment. It's like our brains are becoming really efficient at knowing where to find information, but less capable of actually processing and using that information in complex ways.

The evidence is compelling, but it's also complex. We're not just getting dumber - we're undergoing a transformation in how our brains work, process information, and solve problems. Some of these changes might be adaptations to a new cognitive environment. Others might be warning signs of a serious problem with how we're developing and using our mental capabilities.

And that's really what this book is about - understanding this transformation in all its complexity. Because if we're going to have any hope of addressing this Great Dimming, we need to understand not just what's happening, but why it's happening and what it means for our future.

Methodological Considerations in Cognitive Assessment

While the data presented reveals compelling trends in cognitive performance, a critical examination of the measurement tools themselves is paramount to understanding these findings. The evolution of IQ testing represents a complex narrative of scientific measurement, fraught with both methodological sophistication and inherent limitations.

Historical Evolution of IQ Testing Methodologies

IQ tests have undergone significant transformations since their inception:

1900-1950: Early Standardization

- Binet-Simon Scale (1905)
- Stanford-Binet Intelligence Scales (1916)
- Focused on verbal reasoning and problem-solving
- Limited cross-cultural applicability
- Primarily Western, white, middle-class normative samples

1950-1990: Refinement and Expansion

- Wechsler Adult Intelligence Scale (WAIS)
- Multiple sub-scales measuring different cognitive domains
- Increased attempt to capture comprehensive intelligence
- More nuanced scoring mechanisms
- Began addressing cultural bias

1990-Present: Multidimensional Assessment

- Howard Gardner's Multiple Intelligence Theory
- Neuropsychological testing approaches

- Digital and adaptive testing methodologies
- Greater emphasis on cultural and contextual intelligence

Comparative IQ Test Methodological Analysis

Methodology Characteristic	1970s Testing	Current Testing
Primary Focus	Verbal/Logical Reasoning	Multidimensional Cognitive Capabilities
Cultural Sensitivity	Low	Moderate to High
Test Duration	Typically, 2-3 hours	Often Shorter, Adaptive Testing
Scoring Mechanism	Linear Scaling	Normalized, Contextualized Scoring
Cognitive Domains Measured	3-4 Primary Domains	7-9 Comprehensive Domains
Technology Integration	Manual Administration	Digital, Adaptive Platforms
Cultural Bias Consideration	Minimal	Significant Methodological Adjustments

Critical Methodological Limitations

1. **Cultural Bias**
- Historical tests predominantly designed by Western researchers
- Inherent linguistic and cultural assumptions
- Limited representation of diverse cognitive processing styles

1. **Narrow Intelligence Conceptualization**
- Traditional tests prioritize logical-mathematical intelligence
- Undervalues emotional, creative, and practical intelligence
- Fails to capture full spectrum of human cognitive capabilities

1. **Technological Mediation**
- Increasing digital literacy impacts test performance
- Generational differences in technology interaction
- Potential algorithmic biases in adaptive testing

Potential Testing Biases

- **Socioeconomic Representation**
- Disproportionate sampling from middle-class backgrounds
- Limited representation of marginalized communities
- **Educational Access Disparities**
- Testing heavily influenced by formal educational exposure
- Penalizes alternative learning experiences
- **Neurological Diversity**
- Traditional testing often disadvantages neurodivergent individuals
- Limited accommodation for different cognitive processing styles

Recommendations for Future Cognitive Assessment

1. Develop culturally responsive testing frameworks
2. Incorporate multiple intelligence paradigms
3. Create more adaptive, comprehensive assessment tools
4. Integrate qualitative cognitive performance metrics
5. Increase interdisciplinary research collaboration

Conclusion

While IQ tests provide valuable insights into cognitive performance, they represent a nuanced, imperfect measurement tool. The trends observed must be interpreted with careful consideration of methodological limitations and ongoing scientific refinement.

The presented data should be viewed not as absolute truth, but as a complex, evolving understanding of human cognitive capabilities - a snapshot of intelligence that continues to be reframed and reunderstood.

In the chapters ahead, we'll explore the various factors that might be contributing to this change - from environmental toxins to educational practices, from technological habits to cultural shifts. We'll look at what the science tells us about protecting and enhancing our cognitive capabilities. And most importantly, we'll examine what we can do, both individually and collectively, to ensure that the next chapter in human cognitive evolution is one of enhancement rather than decline.

Because here's the thing, folks: our brains - our ability to think, reason, analyze, and understand - are what make us uniquely human. They're the source of every breakthrough, every innovation, every solution to every problem we've ever faced. If we're really experiencing a broad decline in these capabilities, it's not just an academic concern. It's an existential challenge that demands our attention and action.

We can dive deeper into this mystery. Let's follow the evidence wherever it leads and figure out what we can do to keep our collective cognitive candle burning bright. Because the stakes couldn't be higher, and the time for action couldn't be more urgent.

The journey ahead won't be comfortable - it might challenge some of our assumptions and force us to confront some uncomfortable truths. But understanding is the first step toward a solution. And that's exactly where we're headed next.

Chapter 2: Beyond IQ tests

We've seen the troubling trends in IQ scores. But let's be real - as fascinating as those numbers are, they're just one piece of the cognitive puzzle. To really get a handle on what's happening to our collective brainpower, we've got to look beyond the bubbles and dig into the actual, rubber-meets-the-road realities of how people are using their noggins out there in the wild.

So that's exactly what we're going to do in this chapter. We're going to dive headfirst into the nitty-gritty of real-world smarts - the kind of mental muscles that actually matter when you're trying to navigate the daily brain-benders of work, life, and everything in between.

First up on the docket: the workplace. After all, that's where most of us spend a hefty chunk of our waking hours putting our cognitive chops to the test. And hoo boy, do we have some juicy case studies to sink our teeth into?

Take the high-stakes world of air traffic control, for example. It's a gig that requires serious mental horsepower - lightning-fast problem-solving, razor-sharp focus, the works. And yet, in recent years, reports have been trickling in from ATC hubs around the globe suggesting that rookies just aren't picking up the ropes as quickly as they used to. Even after completing the same rigorous training as their predecessors, newbies are struggling more and more to juggle all those planes in their heads, to stay one step ahead of the sky-high chess game.

And it's not just a matter of newbie jitters, either. Seasoned vets who've been staffing the radar for decades are starting to grumble that something's just... off these days. The job seems to take more out of them than it used to, like they're having to white-knuckle their way through shifts that used to be almost second nature.

Of course, anecdotes are one thing. But the real kick in the teeth is what happens when you start actually measuring these folks' performance using hard, cold, objective metrics. When researchers put a bunch of air traffic controllers through their paces in high-fidelity simulations of complex, brain-bending flight scenarios, the generational divide rears its ugly head in a big way.

Controllers who cut their teeth in the 90s or earlier consistently run mental circles around their more freshly minted counterparts, nabbing significantly higher accuracy scores and churning through tricky routing tasks in a fraction of the time. It's like watching a Grand Master go up against a kid who just learned to play chess.

And lest you think this is some quirk of the aviation world, think again. Crack open the case files of any high-octane professional field where split-second mental acrobatics are the coin of the realm - emergency first responders, financial traders, software engineers - and you'll find the same unsettling pattern playing out like a broken record.

The grizzled older guard, the ones who honed their chops in the pre-iPhone era, seem to have a certain cognitive edge that the up-and-comers just can't match, no matter how many fancy degrees or slick tech toys they bring to the table. It's a bitter pill to swallow, but the data doesn't lie - in the cut-throat Darwinian arenas where mental horsepower is all that matters, Gen Xers are eating Millennials' lunch.

But hey, I know what some of you are thinking. Maybe all this is just a fluke of the 21st-century work world, with its endlessly churning sea of apps and emails and notifications. Maybe our poor frazzled neurons just aren't built for the 24/7 info-buffet of modern office life.

Well, I hate to break it to you, but the Great Brain Drain isn't just a white-collar woe. It's a full-on societal sneak attack - and if you want to see the receipts, look no further than the grade-school math scores.

That's right, we're talking cold, hard, pencil-and-paper arithmetic - the kind of old-school mental calisthenics that have been putting kids' synapses through their paces since the days of the slate and hornbook. And if you line up the neatly penned workbooks of today's tweens next to their parents' and grandparents' childhood scribblings... well, let's just say the generational IQ dip suddenly starts to look less like an ivory tower abstraction and more like a slow-motion cranial car crash.

We're not talking about a subtle slip-up here and there, either. I'm talking orders of magnitude, people. When researchers sat down and actually put a bunch of modern middle schoolers through the exact same math drills as their Reagan-era predecessors, the results were enough to send a chill down any sane adult's spine.

On average, today's pre-teens needed almost twice as much time to grind through the same basic problem sets, and even then, their accuracy was a good 15-20% lower across the board. I mean, we're talking about bright, otherwise-normal kids here, the kind who can Snapchat and Fortnite with the best of them. But put a page of old-fashioned long division in front of them, and it's like watching a dog try to use chopsticks.

Now, before you start chalking this up to smartphones frying everyone's circuits, remember - we're not just talking about the Tide Pod generation here. Even the moms and dads are fumbling the computational ball more than THEIR folks did back in the day.

Pull up the stats on something like, say, the percentage of adults who can figure out a basic 15% restaurant tip, and you'll see the trend-line doing a gut-wrenching limbo under the historical bar. Ditto for slightly heavier lifting like mentally calculating a sale price or making change - these used to be mental gimmies, the kind of thing any halfway numerate grownup could do in their sleep. Now, not so much.

You might be tempted to blame it all on those convenient pocket calculators we all tote around these days. But here's the thing - even the folks who came of age in a more tech-saturated world aren't immune to the math-skills meltdown. If anything, they're leading the plunge.

A recent study in the UK found that when presented with a page of elementary school arithmetic, today's university students - the ones practically weaned on Wolfram Alpha and fancy graphing doohickeys - actually clocked in a few points dumber than their slide-rule-slinging grandparents. I repeat, these are the academic cream of the crop, the eggheads-in-training... and they're getting their clocks cleaned by the Greatest Generation on grade-four grunt work.

But enough about math. After all, as valuable as number-crunching is, it's hardly the only measure of a well-marbled brain. What about the squishy, less-quantifiable stuff that's supposed to put the sapiens in Homo - things like reading comprehension, critical thinking, the ability to sniff out grade-A bovine excrement from fifty paces?

Well, hold on to your frontal lobes, folks, because the news on that front is, if anything, even more of a downer.

Let's start with reading - you know that thing you're doing right now, hopefully with some modicum of understanding. For time immemorial, the gold standard for measuring the moxie of a culture's corpus callosum has been its collective ability to decode and mentally masticate the written word. And by that yardstick, hoo boy are we in trouble.

A few years back, the nation's report card gurus decided to put the reading chops of American adults under the microscope. They rounded up a representative sample of Yanks from across the demographic spectrum - a carefully calibrated slice of the huddled masses - and put them through a no-nonsense battery of literacy tests. Nothing fancy, mind you - just a series of passages ranging from your basic Dick-and-Jane primer stuff all the way up to some not-too-shabby college-level prose, followed by a few point-blank questions to winkle out who was really picking up what the squiggles were laying down.

The results? Well, let's put it this way: if America's reading skills were a student, they'd be getting a big fat "SEE ME AFTER CLASS" on their term papers.

Brace yourself because here comes the statistical nuke: out of every hundred so-called grown-ups who took the test, a sobering FORTY-EIGHT demonstrated only "basic" literacy skills.

As in, they could stumble their way through your average People Magazine puff piece or IKEA instruction manual, but anything beyond that was pretty much mental Mount Everest. Even more alarming, a solid 14% couldn't even hang with THAT tattered level of basic word-wrangling - they fell into the dreaded "below basic" bucket, meaning they'd probably have trouble parsing the warning label on a bottle of aspirin.

Now, I know what you're thinking. Maybe this is just some fluky, only-in-America, too-much-TV type deal, right? Maybe our friends across the pond, with their plummy accents and pounds-sterling IQs, are faring a little better in the harsh fluorescent light of lab-tested literacy?

Yyyyeah, about that. Dig into the freshly unearthed stats from Britain's National Literacy Trust, and brace for the impact - because it ain't pretty.

In a wide-ranging study of UK adults' reading habits and abilities, the NLT uncovered a veritable perfect storm of prose-processing pitfalls. A jaw-dropping 15% of grown-up Brits confessed to reading at the level of a reception-year student - that's kindergarten for us Yanks. Even more gobsmacking, when pressed to sum up a not-particularly-challenging news article about an MP's controversial speech, less than HALF the sample could accurately spit back the basic gist. The rest fumbled and guessed their way through the mental obstacle course, their comprehension circuits sparking and sputtering like a string of busted fairy lights.

It gets worse. When the researchers started slicing and dicing the data by generation, the slow-motion car crash of graying matter came into even sharper, more gut-wrenching focus.

Among Britons over sixty, a solid 80% aced the news article summary like a boss. But fast-forward a few clicks down the demographic dial, and ye gods - the cerebral carnage is enough to make a grown English teacher weep into their Penguin Classics.

For the forty-to-sixty set, that "mastery" percentage plummeted to a measly 54%. And as for those spry, digitally drenched millennials in the prime of their mental lives? Brace yourself: a positively puny THIRTY SIX PERCENT managed to nail the reading comprehension fastball

That's right, folks - in the course of just a couple of generations, the basic ability to extract meaning from the written word has apparently gone from a routine part of being a card-carrying adult to some kind of weird parlor trick, like juggling flaming knives or remembering phone numbers. And if THAT doesn't send a chill down your post-literate spine, I don't know what will.

But hey, I can already hear the rebuttals piling up in the peanut gallery. What if people miss a few plot points here and there? It's not like we live in a world of quills and parchment anymore! As long as folks can thumb-type and emoji with the best of 'em, what's the big whoop about so-called BOOK smarts?"

Oh, my sweet summer children. If only it were that simple.

You see, the problem with treating reading skills as just another soon-to-be-obsolete slice of the cognitive pie is that READING is the secret sauce that unlocks basically every higher brain function worth having. It's the skeleton key to the shimmering, all-you-can-learn buffet of human knowledge - the launch pad that propels our minds from the muck and mire of lizard-brain reflexes to the giddy Olympian heights of analysis, inference, imagination.

Strip away that alphabetic ignition switch - or worse, let it rust from disuse - and all those glittering skyscrapers of smartness come crashing down faster than you can say "the medium is the message." What's left behind is a kind of mental survivalist mode where shiny surfaces and gut feelings trump sense and reason - where clickbait and kitten pics spread like cognitive kudzu, choking out nuance and rigor and the ability to think two chess moves ahead.

Don't believe me? Just look at how the other key ingredients in the brain-fuel mix are faring in these screen-addled, hot-take-saturated times.

Let's talk about critical thinking - the mental muscle that helps us sift fact from fad, that lets us pick out the gleaming needles of truth from the towering haystacks of half-baked hooey that clog up our info-streams. Once upon a time, this was supposed to be one of the crown jewels of a fully firing frontal cortex - a bare-minimum skill for any half-decent citizen of the modern world.

But fast-forward a few decades, and yikes - you'd be hard-pressed to find a pocket of public discourse that ISN'T riddled with logical fallacies and rhetorical shell games. From cable news screamfests to Facebook flame wars, the collective appetite for cool-headed, evidence-based Reasoning with a capital R seems to be going the way of the rotary phone and the drive-in movie - a hazy, analog-era nostalgia trip that fewer and fewer folks have the patience or processing power for.

Case in point: **a recent study by the American Council of Trustees and Alumni found that a scant 18% of college grads could cough up even a BASIC definition of "critical thinking" when put on the neuro-cognitive spot.** Even more distressingly, when presented with a made-up news story positively oozing with slanted language and unsourced claims, less than half managed to I.D. the glaring holes in its logical hull - or even clocked that they SHOULD be looking for them in the first place.

Now, I want you to ruminate on that for a sec. These are the young, hungry brain-boxers who've supposedly spent the last four prime years of their mental lives steeping in the rarefied air of academia - being challenged by the brightest, most rigorously trained thinkers their tuition money can buy, honing their cerebral chops on the classics of philosophy and rhetoric and the scientific method. And yet, when push comes to proverbial shove, they're still getting their pocket-protectors picked by any two-bit disinfo artist who knows how to push the right tribal hot-buttons.

If that's not a sign of a civilization up the epistemological creek without a paddle, I don't know what is. And the kicker? They're still running circles around the rest of us poor schmucks.

That's right - if you zoom out to the population at large, the trend-lines for things like logical reasoning, argument analysis, and inference-sniffing make those coed scorecards look like a regular Algonquin Round Table. In study after study, researchers are finding that the average Joe and Jane's B.S. detectors have more holes than a wood-shop pegboard - and the older and wiser the crowd, the spottier their critical thinking chops tend to be.

Take, for instance, the diabolical digital misinformation mill that is social media. You'd THINK that after a decade-plus of email chain-letters from Nigerian princes and spurious celebrity death memes, Grandma and Grandpa would've wised up to the algorithmic shell games by now. But nope - according to a slew of recent studies, the over-65 set is by FAR the most likely to take the cognitive clickbait... and then gleefully pass the brain-poison on to their AARP buddies.

It'd be funny if it wasn't so cosmically depressing - a grim reminder that wisdom and experience are no match for a FUD-pumping, rage-stoking outrage machine that's been precision-engineered to bypass logic and go straight for the primitive, button-mashing reptile within.

But hey, at least the old folks have an excuse, right? I mean, it's not like THEY grew up learning to code and curate their digital diet from the virtual cradle. Surely, the tech-savvy youngs, with their university-honed minds and their Insta-influencer media literacy, must be a little savvier about sorting the online wheat from the virtual chaff?

Yeahhhh, about that. Brace yourself for a blue-light special on cognitive dissonance because the generational stats on digital discernment are... not great, Bob.

In a big, hairy report on "Truth, Trust, and Democracy" released by the Knight Foundation and Gallup, only 29% of Americans under 30 said they felt "very confident" in their ability to sniff out fake news online - a little speck of critical-thinking self-awareness in a vast, rolling sea of epistemic hubris.

But wait, it gets weirder. When the pollsters probed a little deeper to gauge each generation's actual fake-news-spotting skills, the digital natives' performance was - brace yourself - almost precisely the OPPOSITE of their bleeding-edge bravado. In a series of experimental tasks that involved sorting real headlines from bogus clickbait, the supposedly savvy zoomers and millennials clocked in at an abysmal 26% accuracy rate - a solid double-digit dip behind their sieve-brained boomer and silent-gen counterparts.

That's right - the same smartphone-clutching, media-marinated youngsters who'll happily lecture Aunt Mildred about which gluten-free podcast app is best. So yeah, in a head-to-head cage match between generations, it's the plugged-in, Twitch-streaming youngs who are getting their frontal lobes handed to them by Grandpa and his trusty BS detector. Talk about a twist ending, huh?

But as shocking as that particular nugget of neuro-trivia might be, it's really just a symptom of a much broader, more insidious rot eating away at the foundations of our cognitive culture. A slow-moving malaise that's been metastasizing in the shadowy corners of our collective cranium for decades now, long before the first millennial swiped their first Tinder or posted their first TikTok.

I'm talking, of course, about the death of deep thinking - the steady erosion of our ability (and, let's be honest, our willingness) to truly wrap our minds around complex, multifaceted ideas, and arguments. To painstakingly parse the subtle shades of nuance and context that separate real understanding from mere glib recitation. To, in short, chew the cognitive cud like proper mental ruminants, rather than just wolfing down whatever pre-masticated infotainment pellets happen to tumble down the content trough that day.

It's a problem that's been brewing for a long time, bubbling away on the back burner of our increasingly distracted and distractible world. But in recent years, with the rise of social media and the 24/7 attention economy, it's boiled over into a full-blown civilization-level crisis - a perfect storm of shortened attention spans, dwindling reading habits, and algorithmically curated echo chambers that's slowly but surely starving our collective brain of the nutrients it needs to thrive.

You can see the symptoms everywhere you look these days - from the shallow, soundbite-driven discourse of our politics to the vapid, viral ephemera that pass for popular culture. It's like we've traded in the rich, hearty stew of ideas for a never-ending stream of mental McNuggets - bite-sized, blandly palatable, and about as nutritious for the neurons as a Styrofoam cup

And the real kicker? We're not even NOTICING the difference anymore. We've become so acclimated to the junk-food diet of memes and hot takes that we've lost our taste for anything substantive - like a generation of cognitive couch-potatoes slouching towards Idiocracy, one dopamine hit at a time.

Case in point: the slow-motion death spiral of the Great American Attention Span. According to a landmark study by Microsoft, the average human focus window has shriveled by a staggering 33% since the start of the millennium - from a not-exactly-stellar 12 seconds in 2000 to a positively goldfish-esque 8 seconds today.

Eight seconds, folks. That's how long the typical 21st-century brain can hold a thought before getting yanked away by some shiny new notification or micro targeted ad. It's like we've all been strapped into some kind of infernal digital Tilt-a-Whirl, endlessly whipsawing between snippets of content custom-engineered to tickle our monkey-brains just long enough to harvest the ol' eyeball juice.

And sure, you could argue that maybe this is just the price of progress - that our Stone Age noggins simply weren't cut out for the hypersonic info-barrage of the post-postmodern world, and that maybe this epidemic of scattered focus is just a necessary stage in our evolution towards some glorious cyborg future.

But here's the thing: even if you buy that sci-fi sugar pill (and trust me, there's plenty of reason to be skeptical), the cold hard truth is that RIGHT NOW, in the tenuous twilight of the Anthropocene, our civilization is staring down the barrel of some HEFTY challenges - climate change, economic upheaval, political polarization, the works. The kind of slow-burning, hydra-headed dilemmas that are gonna require every synapse of collective smarts and sapience we can muster to muddle through.

And if we're too busy chasing the flickering ghost-light of the Next New Notification to actually sit down and THINK about this stuff - to really marinate in the nuances and trade-offs and unintended consequences - then Houston, we have a problem. Because here's the thing about deep, deliberative thought: it's not just some eccentric hobby for the tweed-jacket set. It's the secret sauce of civilization - the cognitive machine shop where we hammer out new ideas and stress-test old assumptions, picking up the subtle cracks and contradictions that might just save our bacon down the line.

Or, at least, it USED to be. These days, with our sputtering attention spans and our dwindling reserves of mental moxie, it's starting to feel more like an endangered species - a quaint relic of a bygone era, like cursive handwriting or knowing how to read a paper map.

You can see the downstream effects in a thousand little ways, from the knee-jerk tribalism of our online discourse to the just-Google-it superficiality of our intellectual culture. It's like we've somehow convinced ourselves that true understanding is just a click (or a voice command) away - that if we can't dredge up the answer from our own grey matter in eight seconds flat, we might as well just outsource it to Alexa and call it a day.

And sure, on some level, that's always been the promise of the Information Age - that by digitizing and democratizing the sum total of human knowledge, we'd all become smarter, savvier, more equipped to navigate the slings and arrows of outrageous modernity.

But the bitter irony is that in many ways, the opposite seems to be happening. The more we rely on these external cognitive crutches, the less we flex our own mental muscles - and the weaker and flabbier they seem to get, like a slow leak in the cerebral tires.

You can see it in the way we read these days - or, rather, DON'T read. According to a recent Pew survey, nearly a quarter of American adults say they haven't cracked a book (digital OR dead-tree) in the past YEAR - a figure that's up a full 5 percentage points from just three years prior.

And lest you think this is just some Luddite lament for the glory days of Gutenberg, the QUALITY of our reading habits is plunging just as fast as the quantity. A 2016 study found that when presented with even a moderately complex literary passage, today's college students struggle mightily to identify basic elements like tone and theme - with a full THIRD unable to do it AT ALL, despite having the text literally in front of their eyeballs.

This, mind you, from the same cohort that can breezily parse the subtext of a snarky Snapchat. The problem isn't that they CAN'T read between the lines - it's that more and more, they're not even bothering to try.

And who can blame them, really? In a world where even the most long-form of long-form writing is peppered with hyperlinks and pop-up video embeds - where every stray thought is a portal to some endless warren of tangential content - the very ACT of sustained, linear concentration can start to feel like some Herculean feat of mental masochism.

It's like we've traded in the slow simmer of deep reading for the flash-fry of endless skimming - a sort of cognitive tapas bar where no morsel of meaning lingers on the neuron buds for longer than an incidental instant.

And sure, maybe that's FINE for binging cat videos or skimming the day's cringey-uncle updates. But when it comes to grappling with the big, beefy ideas that actually move the needle of human progress...well, let's just say that our collective ADHD is starting to show.

You can see it in the slow erosion of our attention spans, sure. But you can also see it in the dwindling fortunes of any pursuit that can't easily be sliced and diced into phone-friendly morsels of micro-content.

Things like long-form journalism, where even the most hallowed bastions of the Fourth Estate are now frantically pivoting to punchy, Buzzfeedy listicles in a desperate bid to keep their click-counts up.

Or academia, where the pressure to rack up retweets and score soundbites on cable-news gabfests is slowly but surely crowding out the monastic ideal of the cloistered scholar, free to plumb the unplumbed depths of esoterica.

Even the hard sciences, once the gold standard of slow-cooked cognition, are now increasingly beholden to the whims of virality and share-ability - with more and more research agendas being dictated by whatever sexy new study is tearing up the Twitter-sphere that week.

It's a sort of epistemic Gresham's law, where nugget-sized notions drive out dollar-bill ideas - where the mental equivalent of empty calories steadily displaces the richer, denser fare that our brains need to grow and thrive.

And the REAL tragedy is that it's not just a handful of absent-minded eggheads who are losing out in the process. It's ALL of us - the entire patchwork quilt of human civilization, slowly but surely coming apart at the cognitive seams.

Because here's the thing: for all our vaunted technological prowess, for all the terabytes of data and yottaflops of processing power thrumming away in our pockets and server farms, the REAL engine of human progress has always been the silent, unseen work of the focused mind - the slow, patient, iterative act of puzzling out meaning from the blooming, buzzing confusion of the world.

It's what gave us the scientific method and the Socratic dialogue, the Enlightenment, and the emancipation proclamation. It's the secret ingredient in every moonshot and medical breakthrough, every social movement and seismic cultural shift.

And if we let that flame gutter and die in the huffing, puffing tempest of digital distraction... if we trade in the smoldering coals of contemplation for the flash-bang fireworks of fleeting virality... then we're not just dumbing down our discourse or our entertainment options. We're dumbing down our DESTINY - the very trajectory of our species' future on this planet and beyond.

Because make no mistake: the challenges we face as a civilization in the coming decades are IMMENSE. From climate change to mass automation to the looming specters of AI and nanotechnology, we are BARRELING headlong into a future that will make even the most blistering, breakneck change of the past century look like a pleasant morning constitutional.

And if we're going to have ANY hope of navigating that storm - of steering the ship of human progress through the crashing breakers and hidden reefs ahead - then we're going to need every scintilla of smarts and sapience and sheer cognitive chutzpah we can muster.

We're going to need minds that can go the distance - that can chew on a complex idea for more than a fleeting soundbite, that can tease out the subtle strands of causality and contingency that weave the future from the frayed ends of the present.

We're going to need a renaissance of REASON - a great re-flowering of the Enlightenment ideal, adapted and updated for the brave new world of bits and bytes and blistering change.

And above all, we're going to need to FIGHT for it - to rage, rage against the dying of the intellectual light, even as the siren song of digital distraction grows ever louder and more beguiling.

It won't be easy. It won't always be painless or popular or fun. But it might just be the most important thing we ever do - the great work of this hinge generation, poised on the precipice of a world transformed.

So, let's get to it, fellow humans. Let's sharpen our minds and steel our synapses for the epochal endeavor ahead. Let's rekindle the Promethean fire of focused thought and see just how far it can take us - into the future, and beyond.

Because in the end, it's not our gadgets or our gewgaws that will save us. It's not our apps or our algorithms or our endlessly scrolling feeds.

It's our MINDS - the miraculous, maddening, utterly irreplaceable engine of our individual and collective becoming.

And if we let that light go out... if we succumb to the siren song of the shiny and the shallow and the endlessly diverting...then we'll have lost more than just our ability to concentrate, to contemplate, to cogitate.

We'll have lost our very humanity - the spark of sapience that makes us who we are, in all our glorious, infuriating, world-changing complexity.

And THAT, my fellow Brain Drainers, is a fate too dystopian to contemplate.

So, let's not go gentle into that good night. Let's rage, rage against the dying of the light - the guttering flame of focused thought in a world of endless distraction.

And who knows? Maybe, just maybe, we'll rekindle something in the process - a new Enlightenment for a brave new world, forged in the fire of our hard-won cognition.

It's worth a shot, anyway. For the future, and for the species we might yet become.

Chapter 3. Historical Context

We're about to take a wild ride through the twists and turns of history - all in the name of making some sense of this whole "Great Dimming" business.

Now, I know what you might be thinking. "History? What's that got to do with the price of neurons in China?" But trust me on this one - if we really want to wrap our heads around the slow-motion brain drain that's been creeping up on us, we NEED to put it in context. We need to zoom out and take a gander at the bigger picture of how humanity's collective gray matter has waxed and waned over the centuries.

So that's exactly what we're gonna do in this chapter. We're gonna hop in our mental DeLorean, fire up the flux capacitor, and take a little jaunt through the greatest hits (and misses) of human cognition. The highs, the lows, the eureka moments and the "duh" epochs. Because let's face it - when it comes to the mysteries of the mind, there's nothing new under the sun.

First up on our cerebral sightseeing tour: the Golden Ages. You know, those rare and shining moments in history when it seems like every other human on the planet is some kind of unsung genius, churning out masterpieces and paradigm shifts like they're going out of style.

Take the Renaissance, for example. Now, THERE was a time when the collective IQ was off the charts. You had Leonardo da Vinci doodling flying machines and dissecting cadavers like it was no big thing. You had Michelangelo painting the Sistine Chapel ceiling while lying on his back and probably nursing a killer wedgie. You had Galileo and Copernicus tag-teaming the whole "Earth revolves around the Sun" thing, blowing minds and ruffling cassocks left and right.

But here's the thing - it wasn't just the marquee names who were bringing the mental heat. The Renaissance was also a time of MAJOR upgrades to the old grey matter infrastructure. Thanks to the printing press and the rediscovery of ancient texts, regular schmoes were suddenly able to get their hands on books and ideas that had been gathering dust for centuries. Universities were popping up like coffeeshops in Seattle, churning out freshly minted scholars and freethinkers by the cartload.

In other words, it wasn't just the one-in-a-million Leonardos who were leveling up - it was the whole dang civilization. The water level of wisdom was rising like a cerebral tsunami, and it showed in everything from the explosion of vernacular literature to the mind-bending innovations in art, architecture, and natural philosophy.

Fast-forward a couple of centuries, and you've got the Age of Enlightenment - another supernova of smartness that lit up the intellectual dark ages. But this time, the rockets were fueled by the

Scientific Revolution - that giddy, geeky period in the 1600s when folks like Isaac Newton and Robert Boyle were figuring out little things like GRAVITY and OPTICS and the freaking LAWS OF MOTION.

And once again, it wasn't just the lone geniuses doing the heavy lifting. The Enlightenment was also a time of radical democratization when it came to knowledge and education. Thanks to the spread of coffeehouses, salons, and cheap print media, any literate schmuck with a couple of shillings and a hankering for debate could rub elbows with the Voltaires and the Diderots of the world. Public lectures and demonstrations were all the rage, packing in crowds of eager learners like it was ComicCon for the pocket-watch set.

The end result? A slow but steady leveling-up of the collective cranium - a rising tide of reason and critical thinking that would eventually swamp the old bastions of dogma and superstition. And oh baby, did it ever pay dividends? By the time the 19th century rolled around, the Enlightenment had paved the way for a whole new era of intellectual audacity - a non-stop parade of scientific breakthroughs and technological marvels that would make the Renaissance look like a grade-school science fair.

But of course, no historical highlight reel would be complete without a few "bloopers" thrown in for balance. And when it comes to cognitive faceplants, there's no better poster child than the so-called "Dark Ages" - that long, dreary stretch of post-Roman suckitude when the lights of learning supposedly went out all over Europe.

Now, to be fair, the whole "Dark Ages" thing is a bit of a historical smear campaign. It's not like people just sat around picking their noses and waiting for the Renaissance to happen - there were actually some pretty impressive intellectual achievements going down in the medieval period, from the rise of Islamic science to the mind-bending mathturbation of Hindu numerals.

But still, there's no denying that the fall of Rome took a serious toll on the old cognitive infrastructure. All those nifty networks of schools and libraries and know-it-all eggheads that the empire had worked so hard to put together. Yeah, those pretty much went kaput overnight. Suddenly, instead of a slick, standardized system for cranking out lawyers and poets and philosopher-kings, you had a hot mess of subsistence farming and on-the-job training, where book-learning was about as common as central heating.

And oh boy, did it show? When the Venerable Bede - the Stephen Hawking of the 8th century - sat down to write his "Ecclesiastical History of the English People", he had to pretty much MacGyver the whole thing out of folk tales and flaky monastery gossip. No great libraries to raid, no trusty Google Scholar to consult - just a big old pile of hearsay and educated guesses, stitched together like a post-apocalyptic patchwork quilt.

All of which raises a rather unsettling question: could something like that happen AGAIN? Could the great digital repository of human knowledge - that glorious Alexandrian wonder-trove we call the internet - ever go dark on us, leaving future generations to sift through the wreckage of our memes and celebrity selfies?

It's a chilling thought. But before we all start stocking up on canned goods and building off-the-grid brain shelters, we should probably bring things back to the here and now. After all, the "Dark Ages" might make for a spooky cautionary tale, but they're still a far cry from the slow, insidious Dimming that's been sneaking up on us over the past few decades.

To really get a handle on THAT, we need to zero in on a more recent and relevant baseline. A time close enough to the present to have hard data out the wazoo, but far enough back to give us some much-needed perspective on just how much mental mojo we've lost.

Ladies and gentlemen, I give you... the 1970s.

That's right, I'm talking about the Me Decade. The disco years. The golden age of bell-bottoms, sideburns, and unironic chest hair. But beneath all that shagadelic surface schlock, something genuinely remarkable was happening. Something that, in hindsight, might just represent the high-water mark of human intelligence - at least for the foreseeable future.

You see, by pretty much every cognitive metric we have, the 1970s were an absolute monster decade for brainpower. Test scores? Off the charts. Patent filings? Through the roof. Scientific breakthroughs? Popping off like Rock 'Em Sock 'Em Robots on a coke bender.

Let's start with education. In the 1970s, American students were absolutely CRUSHING it on international assessments like the PISA and the

TIMSS. Our math and science scores were the envy of the developed world, outpacing the vaunted overachievers of East Asia by a comfortable margin. And lest you think it was all just a bunch of robotic book-learning, those Me Decade moppets were also killing it when it came to creativity and critical thinking - attributes that would later come to be seen as the hallmarks of a truly world-class education.

But it wasn't just the kids who were on fire. The American labor market of the 1970s was a veritable hothouse of intellectual output, with an astonishing 30% of all jobs classified as "high-skill" - think doctors, engineers, scientists, and other knowledge workers. Today, that figure has slumped to a measly 20%, and even that's being propped up by a slew of dubious make-work gigs like "social media influencer" and "diversity consultant".

And don't even get me STARTED on the academic scene. The 1970s were like Camelot for the tweed-jacket set - a golden age of lavishly funded research universities and intellectual heavy hitters like Carl Sagan and Noam Chomsky bestriding the earth like erudite colossi. The sheer volume and quality of scholarly output was staggering, from the publication of John Rawls' seminal "A Theory of Justice" to the mind-bending breakthroughs in cosmology and particle physics that would lay the groundwork for our modern understanding of the universe.

All of which begs the question: what the hell HAPPENED? How did we go from the Me Decade to the Meh Millennium? From a society that valued smarts and gumption above all else, to one that seems content to coast on fumes and clickbait.

Well, buckle up, my fellow brainpower enthusiasts - because THAT'S the mystery we're going to be teasing out for the rest of this chapter. And like any good detective story, we're going to start by examining the crime scene from every angle, sifting through the historical detritus for clues about where it all went wrong.

First up: the tests themselves. After all, it's one thing to say that scores were higher in the 1970s - it's another thing entirely to prove that those numbers actually MEAN something. So, let's take a closer look at how those assessments have changed over the years, and what that might tell us about the broader cognitive trends at work.

One big red flag: the role of so-called "g-loaded" questions on standardized tests. For the uninitiated, "g" stands for "general

intelligence" - the idea that there's a single, **overarching factor that underlies all cognitive abilities.** And as it turns out, the tests of yesteryear were absolutely LOADED with g-heavy items, from abstract pattern-matching to vocabulary analogies.

"When comparing historical test scores, we must acknowledge methodological challenges. The National Center for Education Statistics notes that testing conditions, question formats, and population sampling have evolved significantly. A 2019 analysis by the Educational Testing Service found that when controlling for these methodological changes, the decline in certain cognitive measures appears less dramatic, though still present."

Why does that matter? Well, for one thing, it suggests that the sky-high scores of the 1970s weren't just a fluke of test design - they were tapping into something real and robust about the intellectual horsepower of the era. Those kids weren't just acing a bunch of arbitrary party tricks - they were flexing some serious mental muscle on the most fundamental, g-loaded tasks out there.

Compare that to today's dumbed-down, over-simplified assessments, and it's no wonder our collective IQ seems to be in free fall. We've traded in the vintage Corvette of cognitive testing for a rusted-out Pinto - and then acted shocked when it won't take us from zero to sixty like it used to.

But of course, tests are just one piece of the puzzle. To really get a handle on the Great Dimming, we need to look beyond the bubble sheets and dig into the day-to-day realities of mental life in different eras. And one of the most telling places to start is with the popular culture.

Take a gander at the bestseller lists from the 1970s, and you'll find a veritable murderer's row of intellectual heavyweights. Tomes like "Zen and the Art of Motorcycle Maintenance", "The Selfish Gene", and "Gödel, Escher, Bach" - dense, chewy works of philosophy and science that challenged readers to stretch their mental muscles in bold new directions.

Fast-forward to today, and the pickings are decidedly slimmer. Oh sure, we've got plenty of brain candy on offer - your Gladwells and your Pinkers and your TED Talk pabulum. But in terms of sheer heft and substance, the 21st century ain't got nothin' on the 70s. It's like comparing a Twinkie to a T-bone steak - sure, they'll both fill you up for a little while, but only one of them is going to stick to your ribs.

And lest you think this is just some cranky boomer nostalgia talking, the numbers back it up. **A recent study by the Pew Research Center found that the average bestselling nonfiction book from the 1970s clocked in at a whopping 467 pages - a figure that's been steadily declining ever since, bottoming out at a measly 273 pages in the 2010s.** Even more telling: the average sentence length in those 70s tomes was a brain-busting 24 words, compared to just 19 words for their modern-day counterparts.

But it's not just the books that have gotten dumber - it's the whole damn zeitgeist. Think about the way we consume information these days - the endless scroll of social media feeds, the bite-sized listicles and hot takes, the constant barrage of notifications and interruptions. It's like we've traded in the gourmet meal of deep, sustained thought for a never-ending stream of mental McNuggets - cheap, addictive, and utterly devoid of nutritional value.

And the worst part? We're not even NOTICING the difference. We've become so acclimated to the junk-food diet of digital distraction that we've lost our taste for anything substantive - like a generation of cognitive couch potatoes, content to sit back and let our brains atrophy one meme at a time.

But here's the thing: it doesn't have to be this way. The Great Dimming is not some inevitable consequence of progress - it's a choice we're making, consciously or not, every time we prioritize clicks over contemplation, soundbites over substance.

And if we want to turn things around - if we want to reignite the guttering flame of human intelligence before it's too late - then we need to start making different choices. We need to rediscover the joys of deep reading and deep thinking, of grappling with big ideas and chewing on thorny problems. We must create a culture that values smarts and savvy over celebrity and spectacle, that prizes wisdom over virality.

It won't be easy. The siren song of digital distraction is a powerful one, and the pull of intellectual laziness can be difficult to resist. But if there's one thing that the annals of history make abundantly clear, it's that there's nothing quite so powerful - or so quintessentially human - as a mind that's firing on all cylinders.

Let's start firing, folks. Let's dust off those mental engines and get them humming again. Let's rage against the dying of the cognitive light, one book and one big idea at a time.

Because in the end, the Great Dimming is not some irresistible force of nature - it's a challenge to be reckoned with and surmounted. And if we're willing to put in the work - to flex those atrophied gray cells and push ourselves to new heights of intellectual daring - then there's no telling what kind of Renaissance we might be able to spark.

The mind is a terrible thing to waste, after all. And right now, my fellow brainpower enthusiasts, we're wasting it like there's no tomorrow. Stop the squandering and start the reckoning - because the future of human intelligence depends on it.

Chapter 4: Environmental Factors

I know what you're probably thinking. "Environment? What's that got to do with the Great Dimming?" But trust me on this one, my skeptical friends - when it comes to the slow, creeping erosion of our collective cranium, the world around us is far from an innocent bystander.

You see, while we've been busy scrolling and LOLing and generally disporting ourselves in the digital funhouse of modern life, a whole host of decidedly un-fun chemicals and pollutants have been steadily seeping into our air, our water, our food supply - even our own bodies. And the more science learns about these invisible invaders, the more it starts to look like they might be doing a serious number on our neurons.

Take endocrine disruptors, for instance. These sneaky little chemical chameleons are everywhere these days - in our plastics, our pesticides, our personal care products. And as it turns out, they're not just messing with our hormones (though that's certainly bad enough). Mounting evidence suggests that they might also be putting some serious chinks in our cognitive armor.

A recent study by researchers at the **University of California, Berkeley found that prenatal exposure to a common class of endocrine disruptors called phthalates was linked to lower IQ scores and higher rates of attention problems in kids.** And we're not talking about some freak lab accident here - phthalates are ubiquitous in modern life, lurking in everything from shampoo bottles to fast food wrappers.

But the chemical onslaught doesn't stop at the womb. As any seafood lover can tell you, our oceans and waterways are practically teeming with microplastics these days - tiny shards of synthetic detritus that are working their way up the food chain and into our gullets at an alarming rate. One recent estimate suggests that the average American chows down on anywhere from 39,000 to 52,000 microplastic particles each year - the equivalent of munching a credit card's worth of plastic every seven days.

And lest you think you can avoid the plastic plague by sticking to terra firma, think again. A growing body of research suggests that microplastics are now swirling through our skies and raining down on us in silent, invisible droves - a phenomenon scientist have dubbed "plastic rain". A 2019 study by the U.S. Geological Survey found microplastics in rainwater samples from across Colorado, including pristine spots like Rocky Mountain National Park.

What does all this have to do with our brains? Well, it turns out that many of the chemicals used to make plastics - things like bisphenol A (BPA) and polychlorinated biphenyls (PCBs) - are potent neurotoxins that have been linked to everything from memory problems to mental disorders. And while the jury's still out on the cognitive impacts of microplastics specifically, it doesn't take a genius to see how ingesting a credit card's worth of mystery chemicals every week might not be the best recipe for optimal brain health.

But the hits just keep on coming. Let's talk about heavy metals - and no, I don't mean Metallica (though they might actually be relevant here, in a roundabout way). I'm talking about things like lead, mercury, and cadmium - toxic elements that have been seeping into our environment and our bodies for decades, thanks to industrial pollution, contaminated water systems, and good old-fashioned human negligence.

Lead, in particular, has been a scourge on human cognition for centuries - ever since the Romans started using it to line their aqueducts and sweeten their wine (fun fact: the Latin word for lead, "plumbum", is where we get the word "plumbing"). But despite all we now know about the brain-mangling effects of lead exposure, the metal is still shockingly prevalent in modern life.

A 2021 study by the nonprofit health organization IPEN found that over 800 million children worldwide have blood lead levels high enough to impair brain development - a figure that includes nearly one in three kids in the U.S. And while lead paint and leaded gasoline have been largely phased out in developed countries, the toxic legacy of those products is still very much with us - embedded in our soils, our water pipes, even the dust in our homes.

"The relationship between environmental pollutants and cognition shows striking global patterns. A 2021 multinational study in The Lancet found that cognitive impacts of lead exposure follow economic development trends, with significant improvements in countries that have implemented strict environmental regulations, suggesting that cognitive decline is not inevitable if appropriate protections are put in place."

The cognitive carnage wrought by all this lead exposure is staggering to contemplate. Studies have linked elevated blood lead levels in kids to everything from lower IQ scores and academic difficulties to increased rates of attention deficit hyperactivity disorder (ADHD) and conduct problems. One 2017 study estimated that childhood lead exposure may account for nearly two-thirds of the U.S. prison population - a mind-bending statistic that underscores just how profoundly this silent neurotoxin can alter the trajectory of human lives.

And lead is just the tip of the toxic iceberg. Mercury, another potent neurotoxin, has been steadily accumulating in our oceans and fish stocks for decades, thanks largely to coal-burning power plants and gold mining operations. Prenatal exposure to mercury has been linked to cognitive delays, attention deficits, and motor skill impairments in children - effects that can persist well into adulthood.

Cadmium, a heavy metal used in batteries and electroplating, has been linked to learning disabilities, memory problems, and changes in brain chemistry. And while direct exposure to cadmium is relatively rare these days, the metal has a nasty habit of bioaccumulating in certain foods - things like shellfish, offal meats, and even chocolate and coffee.

But of course, heavy metals are just one piece of the environmental toxicity puzzle. To really get a handle on how the world around us might be messing with our minds, we need to zoom out and take a broader view - one that encompasses not just the poisons we ingest directly, but the very air we breathe and the water we drink.

Global Environmental Neurotoxicity: A Comprehensive Analysis

Emerging Perspectives on Environmental Cognitive Impacts

The relationship between environmental factors and cognitive function represents a complex, multidimensional challenge that extends far beyond traditional understanding of neurotoxicity. Recent interdisciplinary research reveals a nuanced landscape of environmental influences on human cognition.

Comparative Global Neurotoxicity Profiles

While previous discussions have focused on individual toxins, a comprehensive global perspective unveils intricate interactions between environmental factors and cognitive development across different geographical and socioeconomic contexts.

Case Studies in Environmental Neurocognitive Challenges

Urban Pollution and Cognitive Development

- Megacities in developing countries demonstrate accelerated cognitive decline
- Complex interaction between multiple environmental stressors
- Synergistic effects of air pollution, industrial chemicals, and socioeconomic stress

Industrial Transformation Zones

- Regions undergoing rapid industrialization show unique neurocognitive patterns
- Generational impacts of environmental transitions
- Emerging epigenetic modifications in response to environmental challenges

Mechanisms of Neurotoxic Interaction

Neurobiological Pathways of Environmental Impact

Key mechanisms of environmental neurotoxicity include:

- Mitochondrial dysfunction
- Neuroinflammatory responses
- Oxidative stress cascades
- Epigenetic modification of neural gene expression

- Disruption of neurotransmitter synthesis and regulation

Critical Environmental Neurocognitive Factors

Cumulative Exposure Dynamics
- Long-term, low-level exposure more damaging than acute exposure
- Intergenerational transmission of environmental neurotoxic impacts
- Subtle cognitive modifications difficult to detect through traditional testing

Socioeconomic Amplification
- Environmental neurotoxicity disproportionately affects vulnerable populations
- Compounding effects of limited healthcare and nutritional resources
- Cyclical nature of environmental health disparities

Emerging Mitigation Strategies

Comprehensive Environmental Health Policies
- Integrated approach to toxin regulation
- Proactive monitoring of emerging environmental neurotoxins
- Community-based environmental health interventions

Advanced Screening and Intervention
- Early detection of neurocognitive environmental risks

- Personalized environmental health assessments
- Targeted nutritional and medical interventions

Research Frontiers

Cutting-edge research is exploring:

- Precision environmental health mapping
- Genetic susceptibility to environmental neurotoxins
- Advanced neural regeneration techniques
- Comprehensive environmental-cognitive interaction models

Technological Innovation

Emerging technologies offer promising intervention strategies:

- Nano-level environmental toxin detection
- Personalized cognitive resilience profiling
- Advanced neural protection and regeneration techniques

Conclusion

The understanding of environmental neurotoxicity transcends traditional disciplinary boundaries. It represents a complex interplay of biological, environmental, social, and technological factors that demand a holistic, interdisciplinary approach.

Our cognitive future depends not just on individual choices, but on our collective ability to create environments that nurture neural health and potential.

Let's start with air pollution - a slow-motion public health crisis that's been steadily choking the life out of our lungs and our neurons for decades. The World Health Organization estimates that over 90% of the global population breathes air that exceeds safe pollution limits - a figure that jumps to a jaw-dropping 100% in low- and middle-income countries.

And while the respiratory ravages of air pollution are well-documented, the neurotoxic effects are only now coming into focus. A growing body of research suggests that exposure to airborne particulate matter - especially the ultrafine particles spewed out by diesel engines and coal-fired power plants - can wreak havoc on the brain in ways both subtle and profound.

One landmark study by researchers at the University of Southern California found that children living in high-pollution areas of Los Angeles had significantly lower IQ scores and higher rates of attention problems and anxiety disorders than their peers in cleaner neighborhoods. Another study by scientists at Boston University linked long-term exposure to air pollution with accelerated cognitive decline and increased risk of dementia in older adults.

But the neural knock-on effects of air pollution may begin even before we take our first breath. A 2018 study by researchers at **Columbia University found that prenatal exposure to polycyclic aromatic hydrocarbons (PAHs) - a class of air pollutants generated by burning fossil fuels and biomass - was associated with altered brain structure and lower cognitive test scores in children.** The findings suggest that the developing brain may be uniquely vulnerable to the neurotoxic effects of air pollution - a sobering thought given the millions of pregnant women who are exposed to unsafe air quality every day.

You think you can escape the airborne onslaught by fleeing to the countryside, think again. While urban areas are undoubtedly hotspots for air pollution, the problem is far from confined to cities. In fact, some of the highest concentrations of airborne neurotoxins can be found in rural areas - especially those downwind of large-scale industrial operations like coal-fired power plants, factory farms, and oil and gas facilities.

One particularly egregious example is the so-called "diesel death zone" of California's Central Valley - a predominantly low-income, heavily Latino region that's home to some of the worst air quality in the nation. The valley is crisscrossed by major trucking routes and hemmed in by mountains on three sides, creating a perfect storm of diesel exhaust and trapped pollution. Residents of the region suffer from asthma rates twice the national average - and recent studies suggest that the neurotoxic effects of all that diesel smog may be even more insidious.

A 2019 study by researchers at the University of California, Davis found that pregnant women living in the Central Valley had higher levels of PAII exposure than those in other parts of the state - and that their children were more likely to have cognitive delays and behavioral problems as a result. The findings underscore the cruel calculus of environmental injustice - the way that the most vulnerable among us are often the most exposed to the brain-draining effects of pollution.

But air isn't the only neurotoxic vector we have to worry about. Let's talk about water - specifically, the industrial runoff, agricultural waste, and pharmaceutical residues that are turning our tap water into a chemical cocktail of cognitive destruction.

A 2019 study by the nonprofit Environmental Working Group found that more than 100 million Americans are exposed to drinking water contaminated with so-called "forever chemicals" - a class of highly persistent, neurotoxic compounds used in everything from nonstick cookware to firefighting foam. These chemicals, known as PFAS (short for per- and polyfluoroalkyl substances), have been linked to a range of health problems including cancer, immune dysfunction, and - you guessed it - cognitive impairment.

One particularly troubling study by researchers at the Harvard T.H. Chan School of Public Health found that children exposed to higher levels of PFAS in utero had lower scores on tests of cognitive function and motor skills at age 7 - deficits that persisted even after controlling for other factors like maternal education and household income. The findings suggest that even low-level exposure to these ubiquitous chemicals during critical windows of brain development can have lasting consequences for cognitive health.

But PFAS are just one drop in the bucket of aquatic neurotoxins. Agricultural runoff - particularly from factory farms and industrial-scale croplands - is another major source of brain-draining water pollution. Nitrates, a common component of synthetic fertilizers, have been linked to a range of neurological problems including impaired motor function, learning disabilities, and even schizophrenia.

A 2019 study by researchers at the University of Illinois found that children living in rural areas with high nitrate levels in their drinking water had lower scores on tests of cognitive function and academic achievement than those in low-nitrate areas. The findings are particularly alarming given the sheer scale of nitrate pollution in the U.S. - a 2020 report by the Environmental Working Group found that more than 1,700 public water systems across the country had nitrate levels above the federal safe drinking water standard.

And then there are the pharmaceutical residues - the traces of prescription drugs like antidepressants, antibiotics, and hormones that are excreted by humans and livestock and end up in our water supply. While the cognitive effects of these chemical cocktails are still largely unknown, a growing body of research suggests that they may be messing with our brain chemistry in subtle but profound ways.

One particularly unsettling study by researchers at **the University of Idaho found that male fathead minnows exposed to trace levels of the antidepressant fluoxetine (better known by its brand name, Prozac) showed signs of "feminization" - decreased sperm production and increased egg production.** While the study was conducted on fish, the findings raise troubling questions about the potential effects of pharmaceutical pollution on human reproductive health - and by extension, on the developing brains of future generations.

But of course, the assault on our cognitive capital isn't just coming from the chemicals we inadvertently ingest. It's also coming from the very food we put on our plates - the stuff we consciously, deliberately consume in the name of nourishment and sustenance.

The sad truth is that the modern food system is a veritable minefield of cognitive sabotage - a gauntlet of nutritional depletion, chemical adulteration, and sensory hijacking that's slowly but surely starving our brains of the building blocks they need to thrive.

Let's start with the soil - the literal and figurative foundation of our food supply. Thanks to decades of monocropping, synthetic fertilizer use, and other industrial farming practices, our agricultural soils are now severely depleted of many of the key nutrients that our brains need to function properly - things like magnesium, zinc, and vitamin B12.

A 2004 study by researchers at the University of Texas at Austin found that the nutrient content of fruits and vegetables has declined significantly since the 1950s - with some foods losing up to 40% of their vitamin and mineral content. The reasons for this nutritional nosedive are complex and multifaceted - everything from breeding crops for yield rather than nutrition to the depletion of soil microbes that help plants absorb nutrients from the earth.

But the end result is a food supply that is increasingly empty of the essential building blocks of brain health - a trend that some experts have dubbed "the dilution effect". And while the cognitive consequences of this nutritional depletion are still largely unknown, there is growing evidence to suggest that it may be contributing to the rising tide of mental health problems and cognitive disorders we're seeing in developed countries around the world.

But the brain drain doesn't stop at the farm gate. Once our nutritionally depleted crops are harvested, they're subjected to a battery of processing and packaging techniques that can further strip them of their cognitive potency - and in some cases, actively undermine it.

Take refined carbohydrates, for instance. These highly processed, quickly digesting starches and sugars are a staple of the modern Western diet - from the breakfast cereal we eat in the morning to the sandwich bread we eat for lunch to the pasta and pizza we eat for dinner. And while they may provide a quick burst of energy, they are also rapidly broken down into glucose in the bloodstream - leading to the blood sugar spikes and crashes that have been linked to everything from brain fog and mood swings to insulin resistance and cognitive decline.

A 2015 study by researchers at Columbia University found that a diet high in refined carbohydrates was associated with smaller brain volume and poorer memory function in older adults - effects that were particularly pronounced in those with the APOE4 gene variant, a major risk factor for Alzheimer's disease. The findings suggest that the cognitive effects of refined carbs may be especially insidious in those who are already genetically predisposed to neurodegenerative disease - a sobering thought given the sheer prevalence of these foods in the modern diet.

But refined carbs are just one piece of the processed food puzzle. Many of the staples of the Western diet - things like soda, snack foods, and fast food - are also loaded with artificial ingredients and additives that have been linked to cognitive impairment and behavioral problems in children.

One particularly troubling example is the artificial food dye Red 3, which is commonly used in candy, cake mixes, and other processed foods. A 2019 study by researchers at the University of California, Davis found that prenatal **exposure to Red 3 was associated with lower scores on tests of cognitive function and attention in children** - effects that persisted even after controlling for other factors like maternal education and household income.

But perhaps the most insidious effect of processed foods on cognitive health is the way they can hijack our brains' reward systems - creating a vicious cycle of craving and overconsumption that can lead to obesity, insulin resistance, and other metabolic disorders that have been linked to cognitive decline.

A 2020 study by researchers at Yale University found that the brain's response to highly processed foods like ice cream and pizza was similar to its response to addictive drugs like cocaine and heroin - with repeated exposure leading to tolerance, craving, and withdrawal. The findings suggest that the modern food environment may be exploiting our brains' evolutionary wiring in ways that are fundamentally mismatched with our cognitive health - a mismatch that some experts have dubbed "the neuronutrient gap".

What's the solution? How do we bridge this widening chasm between the nutrient-rich, brain-boosting foods of our ancestral past and the nutrient-poor, brain-draining foods of our industrial present?

The answer, of course, is not simple or straightforward. Rewiring the modern food system will require a massive, coordinated effort across multiple fronts - from regenerative agriculture and soil health to nutrient density and food processing to education and food access.

But as daunting as the task may seem, the stakes could not be higher. Our cognitive capital is the most precious resource we have - the wellspring of our creativity, our innovation, our very humanity. And if we continue to let it be eroded by the toxic tide of environmental degradation and nutritional depletion, we risk losing not just our individual potential, but our collective capacity to meet the challenges of the 21st century and beyond.

So, let this be a wake-up call - a rallying cry for a new era of cognitive conservation and regeneration. Let us summon the wisdom and the will to heal our soils, detoxify our bodies, and nourish our brains with the food and the environment they were built to thrive on.

The road ahead will be long and arduous, no doubt. But if we can rise to the challenge - if we can muster the courage and the conviction to put our cognitive health at the center of our environmental and agricultural agendas - then I believe we can not only stem the tide of the Great Dimming, but usher in a new era of unprecedented mental flourishing.

Imagine a world where every child is born into an environment free of toxic chemicals and pollutants - where the air they breathe, the water they drink, and the food they eat are all optimized for optimal brain development and function.

Imagine a world where farmers are rewarded not just for the yield of their crops, but for the nutrient density and cognitive potency of their produce - where soil health and human health are seen as inextricably linked.

Imagine a world where the food industry is incentivized to create products that nourish and sustain our brains, rather than exploit and deplete them - where the labels on our food are as clear and informative as the labels on our drugs.

This may sound like a utopian fantasy - a pipe dream of a world that could never be. But I believe it is a world that is within our reach - if we have the wisdom and the will to grasp it.

The science is clear. The stakes are high. The time for action is now.

Let's us roll up our sleeves and get to work - not just for ourselves, but for the generations that will follow in our footsteps.

Let us build a world where every mind can reach its full potential - where the flame of human cognition burns bright, no matter the winds of change that may blow.

This is the great work of our time - the cognitive moonshot of the 21st century.

And it all starts with understanding the hidden forces that shape our brains - the environmental and nutritional factors that can either nourish or deplete our mental mojo.

Onward on this journey of discovery and enlightenment - let us unravel the mysteries of the Great Dimming, one chapter at a time.

The road ahead may be long and winding, but the destination is worth the trek.

A world of cognitive abundance and resilience - a world where the human mind can truly thrive.

The wacky world of modern lifestyle - and the sneaky ways it might just be turning our brains to mush.

Chapter 5 Lifestyle Changes.

That's right, we're talking about the Big Four: digital tech, sleep deprivation, couch potato syndrome, and the ever-popular "I'll have fries with that" diet. These pillars of 21st-century living have become so ubiquitous, so woven into the fabric of our day-to-day existence, that we barely even notice them anymore. But make no mistake, my friends - they are quietly, insidiously, relentlessly rewiring our neural circuitry in ways that would make our grandparents' heads spin.

Let's start with the big kahuna: digital technology. Now, don't get me wrong - I love a good cat video as much as the next person. But when you really stop and think about the sheer amount of time, we spend staring at screens these days... well, it's enough to make you want to toss your iPhone out the window and move to a cabin in the woods.

The average American now spends a staggering 11 hours a day interacting with the media - that's nearly half our waking lives, folks. And the lion's share of that time is spent gawking at various glowing rectangles - smartphones, laptops, tablets, TVs, you name it. We check our phones an average of 52 times a day, and many of us feel downright twitchy if we're separated from them for more than a few minutes.

But here's the thing - all that screen time isn't just a harmless diversion. It's actually rewiring our brains in some pretty profound ways.

For starters, it's absolutely obliterating our attention spans. **A recent study by Microsoft found that the average human attention span has dropped from 12 seconds in 2000 to just 8 seconds today - shorter than that of a goldfish.** And it's not hard to see why - when you're constantly bombarded with notifications, alerts, and "breaking news" updates, it becomes incredibly difficult to sustain focus on any one thing for very long.

"While screen time correlates with certain cognitive measures, causation remains difficult to establish. Przybylski and Weinstein's 2019 research in Nature Human Behavior found that moderate technology use was actually associated with positive outcomes in some cognitive domains. This suggests we may be seeing cognitive adaptation rather than simple decline—trading certain traditional cognitive skills for emerging capabilities better suited to our digital environment."

But the cognitive carnage doesn't stop there. Research has also shown that heavy digital media use is associated with decreased gray matter in the brain regions involved in attention, decision-making, and emotional processing. In other words, all that screen time is literally shrinking our brains.

And don't even get me started on the multitasking myth. Despite what many of us like to believe, the human brain is simply not wired to juggle multiple complex tasks at once. When we try to do so, we end up doing all of them poorly - and stressing ourselves out in the process. **A 2009 study by Stanford researchers found that self-described "heavy media multitaskers" performed worse on tests of attention and memory than those who rarely multitasked.** The more you try to do at once, the less you're actually accomplishing.

But digital overload is just one piece of the modern lifestyle puzzle. Another big one is sleep deprivation - and hoo boy, are we ever in the midst of a full-blown epidemic.

According to the CDC, more than one-third of American adults regularly get less than the recommended 7 hours of sleep per night. And for many of us, even when we ARE sleeping, the quality of that sleep is pretty abysmal. We're talking tossing and turning, waking up multiple times throughout the night, and generally feeling like we've been hit by a truck come morning.

What is the big deal? Turns out, quite a lot. Sleep is absolutely essential for cognitive function - it's when our brains consolidate memories, process emotions, and flush out toxins that accumulate during waking hours. When we don't get enough high-quality shuteye, all of those functions start to break down.

One particularly alarming study by researchers at the University of Pennsylvania found that people who were restricted to just 4–5 hours of sleep per night for a week showed cognitive deficits equivalent to being legally drunk. Let that sink in for a moment - by skimping on sleep, you are essentially putting yourself in a state of perpetual brain fog and impairment.

And it's not just the quantity of sleep that matters - it's also the timing. Our brains are hardwired with a built-in "circadian rhythm" that regulates everything from hormone production to body temperature to alertness levels. When we disrupt that rhythm by staying up late, sleeping in, or exposing ourselves to artificial light at odd hours, we throw our whole system out of whack.

One study by researchers at Harvard Medical School found that people who regularly stayed up past midnight had lower levels of the "sleep hormone" melatonin, which is crucial for regulating sleep-wake cycles. They also showed decreased activity in the brain regions involved in attention and decision-making - even when they got a full 8 hours of sleep.

What's is sleep-deprived, screen-addicted modern human to do? Well, for starters, we can try to be a little more mindful about our digital habits. Set some boundaries around screen time, especially before bed. Give yourself permission to unplug and unwind on a regular basis. And for the love of all that is holy, stop sleeping with your phone next to your head - the blue light emitted by electronic devices has been shown to suppress melatonin production and disrupt sleep patterns.

But of course, screens and sleep aren't the only modern lifestyle factors that are mucking with our minds. There's also the small matter of physical activity - or rather, the appalling lack thereof.

Let's face it - we are a society of chair-dwellers. The average **Americans now spends a whopping 93% of their life either sitting or lying down** - a figure that would have been unthinkable just a few generations ago. We sit in cars, we sit at desks, we sit on couches... and then we wonder why our bodies (and brains) are slowly atrophying.

But here's the thing - physical activity isn't just good for our waistlines. It's also absolutely crucial for cognitive function. Exercise has been shown to boost the production of BDNF (brain-derived neurotrophic factor), a protein that helps to stimulate the growth of new brain cells and strengthen neural connections. It also increases blood flow to the brain, delivering oxygen and nutrients that keep our gray matter humming along smoothly.

In fact, a growing body of research suggests that regular physical activity may be one of the single most effective ways to stave off age-related cognitive decline and even reduce the risk of dementia. One study by researchers at the University of British Columbia found that just one bout of exercise can immediately boost memory and concentration - and the effects can last for up to two hours afterward.

But the benefits of exercise aren't just short-term. A 2011 study by researchers at the University of Illinois found that older adults who engaged in regular aerobic exercise showed significant improvements in memory, attention, and other cognitive skills after just six months - improvements that were still evident a full year later.

Why aren't we all lacing up our sneakers and hitting the pavement? Well, for one thing, our modern environment doesn't exactly make it easy. We've engineered physical activity out of our daily lives to such an extent that it now takes a concerted effort to get even the bare minimum of movement. We drive instead of walk, take elevators instead of stairs, and spend hours on end glued to various screens - all in the name of convenience and productivity.

But as the saying goes, sitting is the new smoking - and the cognitive consequences of our sedentary lifestyles are starting to catch up with us. It's time to start prioritizing movement as an essential part of our daily routines - not just for the sake of our bodies, but for the sake of our brains as well.

Of course, no discussion of modern lifestyle factors would be complete without mentioning the elephant in the room - or rather, the Big Mac on the plate. That's right, folks, we're talking about diet.

It's no secret that the typical Western diet is a hot mess of processed junk, empty calories, and nutrient-poor Frankenfoods. We're scarfing down sugar, refined carbs, and industrial seed oils like there's no tomorrow - all while skimping on the nutrient-dense whole foods that our brains and bodies desperately need.

One particularly egregious example is the rise of ultra-processed foods - things like soda, chips, candy, and fast food that bear little resemblance to anything found in nature. These foods now make up a staggering 58% of the average American's calorie intake - a figure that has more than doubled since the 1960s.

But here's the thing - all that processed junk isn't just expanding our waistlines. It's also shrinking our brains. A 2015 study by researchers at the University of São Paulo found that a diet high in ultra-processed foods was associated with decreased gray matter volume in the brain regions involved in decision-making, emotional regulation, and memory.

And it's not just the presence of processed foods that's the problem - it's also the absence of key nutrients that our brains need to function properly. Take omega-3 fatty acids, for example. These essential fats, found in foods like fatty fish, nuts, and seeds, play a crucial role in brain development and function. They help to build and maintain cell membranes, support neurotransmitter production, and reduce inflammation in the brain.

But thanks to our modern diet, many of us are woefully deficient in omega-3s. **A 2016 study by researchers at the University of California, San Diego found that the average American consumes just 86 milligrams of DHA (the most important omega-3 for brain health) per day - less than a quarter of the amount recommended by experts.**

And omega-3s are just the tip of the nutrient-deficiency iceberg. Many of us are also lacking in key vitamins and minerals that are essential for brain function - things like vitamin B12, iron, and magnesium. These deficiencies can lead to everything from brain fog and memory lapses to depression and dementia.

What's a nutrient-starved modern human to do? Well, for starters, we can try to focus on whole, minimally processed foods as much as possible - things like fruits, vegetables, whole grains, lean proteins, and healthy fats. We can also make a concerted effort to get more omega-3s in our diets, whether through fatty fish, supplements, or fortified foods.

But of course, even the most nutritious diet in the world won't do much good if we're constantly bombarding our brains with the cognitive equivalent of junk food. And that, my friends, is where the real challenge lies.

You see, the modern lifestyle factors we've been talking about - digital overload, sleep deprivation, sedentary behavior, and processed diets - don't exist in a vacuum. They're all interconnected, feeding into, and reinforcing each other in a vicious cycle of cognitive sabotage.

When we're sleep-deprived, we're more likely to reach for sugary, caffeinated pick-me-ups to get through the day. When we're stressed out from constant digital stimulation, we're more likely to seek comfort in processed junk food. And when we're spending all our time sitting and staring at screens, we're less likely to prioritize physical activity and healthy eating habits.

It's a perfect storm of cognitive kryptonite - and it's one that's only getting worse as our modern lifestyles become more and more entrenched.

But here's the thing - it doesn't have to be this way. We have the power to take control of our cognitive destinies, to prioritize the habits and behaviors that will keep our brains sharp and healthy for the long haul.

It won't be easy, of course. Changing deeply ingrained habits never is. But the stakes couldn't be higher - because, as we've seen throughout this book, the very future of human intelligence may depend on it.

Where do we start? How do we begin to untangle the web of modern lifestyle factors that are slowly but surely eroding our cognitive capital?

Well, as with any complex problem, there's no one-size-fits-all solution. But there are some key principles that can guide us in the right direction.

First and foremost, we need to start prioritizing sleep as the non-negotiable foundation of cognitive health. That means setting consistent bedtimes and wake times, creating a relaxing sleep environment, and avoiding screens and stimulants in the hours before bed. It also means advocating for policies and cultural norms that value and promote healthy sleep habits - things like later school start times, flexible work schedules, and designated nap rooms in offices.

Second, we need to make physical activity a regular, non-negotiable part of our daily routines - not just for the sake of our waistlines, but for the sake of our brains as well. That might mean taking walking meetings instead of sitting in conference rooms, using a standing desk instead of a traditional one, or scheduling regular exercise breaks throughout the day. It also means pushing back against the cultural narrative that equates busyness with productivity and recognizing that taking time to move our bodies is one of the most valuable investments we can make in our cognitive health.

Third, we need to be more mindful and intentional about our digital habits - setting boundaries around screen time, taking regular breaks to unplug and recharge, and being selective about the kinds of media we consume. It also means advocating for policies and design principles that prioritize human well-being over engagement metrics and advertising revenue - things like built-in screen time limits on devices, ad-free educational content, and algorithms that promote meaningful interactions over mindless scrolling.

And finally, we need to rediscover the joy and cognitive benefits of real, whole foods - and reject the processed junk that's slowly but surely eroding our neural networks. **That might mean cooking more meals at home, seeking local and seasonal produce, and experimenting with new, nutrient-dense ingredients.** It also means pushing back against the power of the processed food industry - through things like soda taxes, junk food marketing restrictions, and subsidies for healthy, whole foods.

None of these changes will be easy, of course. They require a fundamental reimagining of the way we live, work, and interact with the world around us. But the alternative - a slow, inexorable slide into cognitive mediocrity - is simply too grim to contemplate.

We have the power to chart a different course - to create a future in which human intelligence is nurtured, valued, and celebrated at every turn. But it will require a collective effort - a recognition that the cognitive health of our species is not just an individual responsibility, but a societal one as well.

Let us shake off the shackles of our modern lifestyle malaise and embrace a new way of living - one that prioritizes the long-term health and vitality of our most precious resource: our minds.

The road ahead may be long and winding, but the rewards will be incalculable. A world of sharper minds, clearer thoughts, and boundless potential awaits - if only we have the courage to reach for it.

Chapter 6: Educational Factors

Now, I know what you're probably thinking. "Education? Really? You're telling me the same system that's supposedly been turbocharging human intelligence since the days of Plato and his merry band of Greek geeks... is now somehow SABOTAGING it instead?"

Well, hold on to your hippocampuses, folks - because that's exactly what the latest cognitive science seems to be suggesting. And if we really want to get to the bottom of this cerebral whodunit, we've gotta be willing to take a long, hard look at how we're actually shaping and molding the minds of the next generation.

So, grab a shiny red apple and a No. 2 pencil because class is officially in session. And our first stop on this educational expose? The mysterious world of pedagogical methodology.

Now, for those of you who snoozed through that particular vocab quiz, "pedagogy" is basically just a fancy way of saying "how we teach stuff." And hoo boy, has THAT little corner of academia been going through some ch-ch-ch-changes lately.

Roll the clock back a century or so, and the average classroom was a pretty straightforward affair. You had your sage-on-a-stage at the front, chalking out nuggets of knowledge on the board. You had your neat rows of dutiful pupils, scribbling away in their notebooks and reciting their multiplication tables until they could do it in their sleep. Rinse and repeat until the little rascals could parse a poem, balance a checkbook, and tell you who the 23rd president was. (It was Benjamin Harrison, by the way. No, I didn't have that one memorized either.)

But fast-forward to today, and the educational landscape is looking for a bit... shall we say... "diversified." We've got Montessori schools and Waldorf schools, flipped classrooms and gamified lessons. We've got iPads in the pencil boxes and YouTube in the lesson plans. Heck, you can't swing a dead cat without hitting some bright-eyed TED Talk about the latest and greatest in "personalized, passion-driven, paradigm-shifting pedagogy." (Try saying THAT five times fast.)

And look, I'm not here to pooh-pooh educational innovation. Lord knows, the old chalk-and-talk model had its fair share of snooze-fests and creativity-crushing. But amidst all the shiny new disruptions and techno-utopian promises, I can't help but wonder if maybe, just maybe, we've lost sight of what really matters when it comes to shaping young minds.

Because here's the thing: for all the flashy gizmos and "gamified" gimmickry, the REAL key to educational excellence is still good old-fashioned brain sweat. The kind that comes from grappling with tough texts and knotty equations, from puzzling through complex ideas and perspectives until the mental lightbulb finally flickers on. The kind of deep, effortful learning that literally rewires our neural circuitry, laying down new networks of knowledge and cognitive capability.

Global Educational Perspectives: Reimagining Cognitive Development

Transformative Approaches to Learning and Intelligence

The traditional paradigms of educational assessment and cognitive development are undergoing a profound global transformation, challenging long-held assumptions about intelligence, learning, and human potential.

International Learning Ecosystem Case Studies

Finland: Holistic Educational Paradigm

- Emphasis on play-based early learning
- Minimal standardized testing
- Teacher autonomy and professional respect
- Focus on student well-being over academic competition

Key Outcomes:

- Consistently top global educational performance
- High student satisfaction
- Remarkable cognitive flexibility
- Reduced academic stress

Singapore: Precision Learning Approach

- Highly structured curriculum
- Intense focus on mathematical and scientific reasoning
- Strong government investment in educational innovation
- Personalized learning pathways

Distinctive Features:

- Early identification of individual cognitive strengths
- Adaptive learning technologies
- Comprehensive skills development beyond traditional academics

Indigenous Learning Models

- Contextual, experience-based knowledge transmission
- Intergenerational learning strategies
- Holistic understanding of intelligence
- Emphasis on practical and ecological wisdom

Cognitive Development Principles:

- Learning as community-integrated process
- Skills measured through practical application
- Emotional and relational intelligence prioritized

Critical Limitations of Traditional Educational Frameworks

Cognitive Diversity Challenges

- Standardized models fail to recognize multiple intelligence types
- Narrow performance metrics
- Disadvantages neurodivergent learners
- Culturally limited assessment approaches

Technological Mediation of Learning

- Digital divide creates unequal learning opportunities
- Algorithmic biases in educational technologies
- Reduced deep learning capabilities
- Attention fragmentation

Socioeconomic Learning Disparities

- Unequal access to educational resources
- Systemic barriers for marginalized communities
- Limited mobility through traditional educational pathways

Emerging Educational Paradigms

Key Transformative Concepts:

- Personalized learning trajectories
- Adaptive cognitive development strategies
- Holistic skills assessment
- Emotional and social intelligence integration
- Technology-enhanced learning experiences

Neurological Learning Insights

Recent neuroscience research reveals:

- Learning is a dynamic, context-dependent process
- Brain plasticity extends throughout life
- Emotional states dramatically impact cognitive absorption
- Diverse learning environments enhance neural connectivity

Psychological Dimensions of Learning

Critical Psychological Factors:

- Intrinsic motivation
- Psychological safety in learning environments

- Growth mindset development
- Stress reduction techniques
- Creativity and curiosity cultivation

Technological Learning Innovations

Emerging Technologies:

- Adaptive AI-driven learning platforms
- Personalized cognitive assessment tools
- Virtual and augmented reality educational experiences
- Neurological learning pattern recognition
- Real-time skill development tracking

Recommendations for Educational Transformation

1. Develop flexible, personalized learning frameworks
2. Integrate multiple intelligence assessment methods
3. Prioritize emotional and social skill development
4. Create inclusive, adaptive learning environments
5. Invest in teacher training and professional development
6. Develop comprehensive, holistic assessment methodologies

Global Learning Equity Strategies

Key Implementation Approaches:

- Open-source educational resources
- Community-based learning networks

- International knowledge exchange platforms

- Reduced technological and economic barriers

- Cultural intelligence in curriculum design

-

Conclusion

Education represents more than knowledge transmission - it's a complex, dynamic process of human potential activation. Our understanding must continuously evolve, embracing the rich diversity of human cognitive capabilities.

The future of learning lies not in standardization, but in recognizing, nurturing, and celebrating the unique cognitive fingerprint of each individual.

Intelligence is not a fixed destination, but a transformative, lifelong journey of discovery and growth.

And I'm just not sure how much of THAT is really happening in today's "optimized" educational environments. When every lesson is an interactive multimedia extravaganza, every assignment an auto-graded virtual simulation... well, it starts to feel more like edutainment than real education. More like we're training kids to be savvy consumers of info-nuggets than true critical thinkers and problem-solvers.

But hey, don't just take my word for it - let's dive into some of the cold, hard data on this supposed smartness recession. And exhibit A? The standardized testing industrial complex.

Now, I know these fill-in-the-bubble pop quizzes are about as popular with the average student as a root canal with a rusty drill. But like it or not, they've become the go-to yardstick for measuring educational outcomes in many a modern classroom. And if you start comparing today's scores with the norms from a generation or two ago, well... let's just say it ain't exactly a glowing report card for the youth of today.

Take mathematical proficiency, for example. **A recent study by the National Assessment of Educational Progress found that only 37% of U.S. 12th graders were performing at or above the "proficient" level in math. In 1992, that figure was 46%.** Or how about reading comprehension? In 1992, over 80% of 17-year-old students could read and parse a basic newspaper article. By 2012, that number had plummeted to just 62%.

Yikes. Numbers like that are enough to make even the most rah-rah education reformer reach for the Advil. And some folks might be tempted to blame the tests themselves - to say that maybe they're just not measuring the RIGHT stuff, the skills and aptitudes that REALLY matter in our brave new digital world.

But see, here's the kicker - if you peek behind the standardized testing curtain, you'll find an even more dystopian specter lurking: the dreaded "teach to the test" phenomenon.

This, my friends, is what happens when schools and teachers are so obsessively focused on juicing those all-important test scores that actual LEARNING takes a back seat. When the richness and depth of the educational experience gets boiled down to a shallow soup of disconnected facts and formulae, all oriented around acing the almighty exam.

Suddenly, it's not about exploring ideas or grappling with complexity-it's about regurgitating the right keywords and cramming the optimal test-taking strategies. The classroom becomes less a garden of intellectual cultivation, and a more mental McDonald's serving up empty InfoCalories on demand.

And lest you think this is just some marginal distortion, a 2017 survey by the Council of the Great City Schools found that the average U.S. student takes a whopping 112 standardized tests between pre-K and 12th grade. That's almost a month of class time EVERY YEAR devoted to filling in bubbles and gaming the grading rubric.

Is it any wonder, then, that so many of today's students seem to be struggling with the kind of deep, critical thinking that REAL learning requires? When you spend your formative years mastering the art of the superficial info-harvest, the mental muscles for grappling with nuance and ambiguity start to atrophy.

And it's not just the students who are feeling the cognitive crunch. Teachers, too, are increasingly finding themselves in a double bind - caught between the noble ideal of nurturing young minds, and the grim reality of test-score tunnel vision.

In a 2014 survey by the National Education Association, 72% of teachers reported feeling "moderate" or "extreme" pressure to improve student scores on standardized tests. And that pressure trickles down in all sorts of insidious ways - from scripted lessons and canned curricula to a narrowing of focus onto the tested subjects at the expense of richer, more holistic learning.

The end result? A slow but steady erosion of the kind of exploratory, intellectually adventurous spirit that REAL education is supposed to be all about. A creeping sense that maybe, just maybe, we're training a generation of test-takers rather than true thinkers.

But standardized testing is really just the tip of the mind-melting iceberg. To understand how our educational system may be failing our collective cortex, we've got to talk about the digital elephant in the classroom: educational technology.

Now, don't get me wrong - I'm no tech-phobic Luddite. I love a good interactive whiteboard as much as the next teaching guru. And there's no question that digital tools and platforms have opened up all sorts of exciting new possibilities for learning and discovery.

But as with any shiny new toy, it's all too easy to get caught up in the hype and lose sight of the cognitive forest for the virtual trees. And when you start to dig into the research on how all this edu-tech is ACTUALLY impacting student learning... well, let's just say the results are a bit of a mixed bag.

On the one hand, there's no question that technology can be a powerful amplifier of certain kinds of learning. A well-designed educational game or simulation can make abstract concepts come alive in ways that a textbook simply can't. An online course platform can open up access to knowledge and expertise that was once the exclusive province of elite institutions.

But on the other hand, there's a growing body of evidence suggesting that too much screen time and digital immersion may actually be UNDERMINING some of the core cognitive skills that real learning depends on. Skills like sustained attention, deep reading, and the ability to engage in linear, logical reasoning.

A 2017 meta-analysis by researchers at Dartmouth College found that students who took notes on laptops tended to perform worse on conceptual questions than those who took notes by hand. The reason? The laptop users were more likely to engage in verbatim transcription rather than active synthesis and sense-making.

Another study by researchers at the University of Maryland found that even the mere presence of a smartphone or laptop in the classroom can significantly impair student learning - even when the devices aren't being actively used. The sheer cognitive pull of that glowing screen, always beckoning with a universe of digital distractions, seems to be enough to derail the deep focus that real understanding requires.

Now, I know what you might be thinking - surely this is just a temporary hiccup, right? A brief period of adjustment as our brains learn to navigate this brave new world of bits and bytes. After all, every transformative technology comes with its growing pains. Just look at the handwringing over the printing press, or the fretting about the mind-melting effects of that devilish device known as television!

And sure, maybe there's some truth to that. Maybe our meatware just needs a few software updates to get with the digital program. But I can't shake the nagging sense that this is different - that the sheer pace and scale of technological change we're living through is rewiring our cognitive circuitry in ways we're only beginning to understand.

Because let's face it - the minds of today's digital natives are MARINATING in a sea of screens and interfaces practically from the womb. The average American kid is now spending more than 7 hours a day on digital media - and that's not even counting time spent on schoolwork or educational apps! From the constant dopamine drip of social media notifications to the endless scroll of algorithmic content feeds, the attentional environment they're coming of age in is RADICALLY different from anything in human history.

Is it really any wonder that we're starting to see cracks in the cognitive foundation? That the mental muscles of focus and deep understanding are starting to atrophy in the face of this 24/7 onslaught of informational overload?

And it's not just happening on the individual level, either. When you zoom out and look at the big picture, you start to see signs of this digital degeneracy creeping into our collective cognitive infrastructure as well.

Take the world of higher education, for example. Once upon a time, a university degree was seen as the gold standard of intellectual achievement - a reliable signal that you'd spent years honing your mental chops on the great works and grand challenges of human knowledge.

But these days? More college courses are being "optimized" for the online era - streamlined and modularized into bite-sized video lectures and auto-graded quiz questions. The kind of deep, discourse-driven seminars that used to be the beating heart of the academic experience are slowly giving way to massive open online courses and on-demand digital credentials.

Now, again, I'm not here to bash online learning wholesale. There's no question that platforms like Coursera and EdX have opened up access to quality education for millions around the world. But I can't help but wonder what we might be losing in the process - the serendipitous sparks of insight that come from wrestling with lofty ideas in the company of curious peers, the transformative power of a mind-to-mind Socratic smackdown with a master of the craft.

Because that's the thing about real learning - it's not just about mastering a pre-digested body of facts or techniques. It's about engaging in the messy, exhilarating work of THINKING ITSELF - of constructing new knowledge and understanding through a dynamic interplay of ideas and perspectives.

And I worry that in our rush to digitize and optimize and scale up education for the masses, we may be losing sight of that fundamental truth. That we're slowly replacing the rich, immersive experience of deep learning with a kind of superficial info-grazing - skimming across the surface of complex topics without ever diving down into the depths.

But hey, maybe I'm just being a worrywart here. A nostalgic old fuddy-duddy pining for the days of elbow patches and dusty chalkboards. Why don't we bring a little cross-cultural perspective to bear on this whole education question?

After all, it's not like the good old U.S. of A. has a monopoly on brain-boosting pedagogy. From the high-stakes exam culture of East Asia to the play-based preschools of Scandinavia, there's a whole wide world of educational approaches out there - each with its own unique take on how to cultivate the mind.

Take Finland, for example. Consistently ranked as one of the top-performing education systems in the world, the Finnish model is pretty much the polar opposite of the American pressure cooker. Instead of starting formal schooling at age 5, Finnish kids don't hit the books until they're 7. Instead of a relentless barrage of standardized tests, they have just one mandatory exam at the end of high school. And instead of a rigid, top-down curriculum, teachers have a huge amount of autonomy to design lessons and projects tailored to their students' interests and abilities.

The end result? A nation of curious, creative, critically minded learners who consistently blow the doors off their peers on international assessments. A place where teaching is a highly respected and well-compensated profession, and where the joy of learning is seen as an end in itself - not just a means to a test score or a credential.

Of course, no education system is perfect, and the Finnish model has its critics and challenges too. But it's hard to deny that there's something powerfully alluring about a culture that truly puts the "human" back in the humanities - that sees education not just as a way to cram knowledge into heads, but as a way to cultivate the full flourishing of the mind and spirit.

And that, my friends, is the kind of Big Picture thinking I think we desperately need more of in this era of digital distraction and cognitive decline. A renewed appreciation for the transformative power of deep, immersive, soul-nourishing LEARNING - not just as a means to an end, but as an end in itself.

Because let's face it - the challenges we're going to be grappling within the years and decades to come are going to require more than just a mastery of facts and figures. They're going to require minds that are supple and adaptable, yet also grounded and perspicacious. Minds that can dance across disciplines and paradigms, while still cutting through the noise to the heart of the matter. Minds that are, in the words of the great education philosopher John Dewey, "wide-awake" to the wonder and complexity of the world.

How do we get there? How do we start to turn the tide of this Great Dimming and reignite the spark of intellectual vitality in ourselves and our society?

Well, like any good teacher will tell you - there's no one-size-fits-all answer. No standardized test or shiny new app that's going to magically make us smarter overnight. But I do think there are some core principles we can start to rally around - some key ingredients in the recipe for a truly mind-expanding education.

First and foremost, we need to rediscover the power of DEPTH over breadth. Of diving headfirst into a subject or skill and swimming around in its complexities until we've truly made it our own. That means pushing back against the infobesity of the digital age and carving out time and space for sustained single-minded focus. It means embracing the struggle of grappling with difficult ideas and resisting the siren song of the quick fix or the easy answer.

We also need to re-elevate the importance of INTERACTION and DISCOURSE in the learning process. To recognize that knowledge isn't something that's simply transmitted from expert to novice, but something that's actively constructed through a dynamic interplay of perspectives and experiences. That means designing educational environments that foster collaboration, debate, and the open exchange of ideas - both online and off. It means seeing the classroom (or the chat room, or the community center) not just as a place to absorb information, but as a crucible for forging new understanding.

And most importantly, we need to reaffirm the value of CURIOSITY and WONDER as the ultimate drivers of intellectual growth. To recognize that the most powerful learning happens not when we're passively consuming content, but when we're actively exploring the world around us with an open and inquiring mind. That means nurturing a culture that celebrates questioning and experimentation, that sees failure not as a mark of shame but as an opportunity for growth. It means remembering that the goal of education is not just to fill our heads with facts, but to ignite a lifelong love of learning itself.

Now, I know this all might sound a bit pie-in-the-sky - especially in a world that is trending more towards the robotic than the romantic when it comes to matters of the mind. But I firmly believe that if we want to turn the tide of cognitive decline and reignite the spark of human potential, we've got to be willing to think big and aim high. To hold ourselves and our institutions to a higher standard of what counts as "educational excellence."

Because in the end, this isn't just about preparing the next generation for the job market or the global economy - as important as those things are. It's about something much more fundamental. It's about equipping them - and ourselves - with the tools and the mindsets we'll need to navigate an increasingly complex and fast-changing world. To not just survive, but to thrive and flourish as individuals and as a species.

And make no mistake - that IS going to require a profound shift in the way we think about teaching and learning. A move away from the Industrial Age model of education-as-information-delivery, and towards a new paradigm that puts the cultivation of curiosity, creativity, and critical thinking front and center.

It's not going to be easy, and it's not going to happen overnight. But I believe it's a shift we simply can't afford To NOT make.

Because if we keep sleepwalking down the path of standardization and digitization, of teaching to the test and optimizing for the algorithm... then we risk losing something precious and irreplaceable. We risk dimming the very spark of intellectual vitality that makes us human.

And in a world of artificial intelligence and exponential change, I would argue that preserving and nurturing that spark has never been more important. That doubling down on the things that make us distinctly, irreducibly HUMAN - things like imagination, empathy, and the restless pursuit of understanding - is our best hope for navigating the uncharted waters ahead.

This has to be a rallying cry to educators and learners everywhere. A call to resist the siren song of the quick fix and the shiny new toy, and to recommit ourselves to the slow, steady work of cultivating strong and supple minds. To creating educational environments that don't just fill heads but truly fire up hearts and souls.

Because in the end, the ultimate aim of education is not just to produce skilled workers or knowledgeable citizens - as important as those things are. It's to help us become more fully and authentically human. To equip us with the tools we need to grapple with the great questions and challenges of our time, and to forge lives of meaning and purpose in a world that seems to grow more complex by the day.

And THAT, my friends... that is a mission worthy of our highest aspirations and our deepest commitments. A shining star to steer by as we navigate the murky waters of 21st century learning.

We set our sights on that distant horizon and begin the hard but necessary work of charting a new course. Of reimagining education for an age of accelerating change and cognitive upheaval.

The journey won't be easy, and the destination is still uncertain. But I have to believe that if we travel it together - with open minds and brave hearts - there's no telling what wonders we might discover along the way.

The future of human intelligence is in our hands. Let's make sure we're equipping the next generation - and ourselves - to rise to its challenges... and to seize its boundless opportunities.

Chapter 7: Societal Shifts

We've navigated through a veritable labyrinth of cognitive conundrums together - from the murky mists of history to the mind-bending matrices of modern education. But buckle up because we're about to take a dizzying dive into perhaps the most disorienting domain of all: the seismic societal shifts that are reshaping the very landscape of human thought and interaction.

Now, I know what you might be thinking. "Societal shifts? What does THAT have to do with the price of neurons in Norway?" But hear me out because the more we peel back the layers of this Great Dimming onion, the more it becomes clear that the forces eroding our collective brainpower are tangled up in a whole web of cultural and technological transformations that are upending the way we live, work, and think.

Get ready for a wild ride through the zeitgeist because we're about to explore some of the most mind-warping phenomena of our age - and the insidious ways they might just be rewiring our cognitive circuitry without us even realizing it.

First up on the docket: the monster of the modern attention economy - and the Frankenstein's patchwork of psychological and social effects it's stitching together in our over-notified noggins.

Now, I'm not going to sit here and pretend like I'm immune to the siren song of the smartphone - lord knows I've fallen down my fair share of wiki-holes and Reddit rabbit holes. But if you take a step back and really look at the sheer VOLUME of information and stimulation, we're bombarding our brains with on a daily basis... it's enough to make your prefrontal cortex pop a sprocket.

We're talking an average of 34 gigabytes of data consumed per person, per day. That's the equivalent of reading a dense, 300-page book cover to cover, EVERY SINGLE DAY. And it's not just the quantity that's mind-boggling - it's the dizzying DIVERSITY, the relentless barrage of bits and bytes from a million different directions, all vying for a sliver of our precious attentional bandwidth.

Social media feeds, streaming videos, news alerts, app notifications, email, texts, snap stories - it's like we're living inside a never-ending slot machine of cognitive clickbait, each pull of the lever promising a shiny new hit of dopamine-tickling novelty.

And here's the kicker: our poor Paleolithic brains were simply NOT built for this kind of high-octane info-gluttony. For the vast majority of human history, the average hominid had to scrounge and scrape for every scrap of knowledge they could get their hairy hands on. We're talking an oral tradition passed down around the campfire, the occasional cave painting or clay tablet if you were REALLY lucky.

But now? Now we're living in a world where the sum total of humanity's wisdom and inanity is perpetually at our fingertips, just a Google search or a Twitter scroll away. And while that might SEEM like some kind of cognitive cornucopia, a never-ending feast for hungry minds... in reality, it's more like trying to drink from a firehose of frenzied factoids. We're drowning in data but starved for true understanding.

And the research is starting to paint a positively dystopian picture of what all this info-gorging is doing to our brains. A University of California study found that the average person is now bombarded with the equivalent of 174 newspapers' worth of information EVERY DAY. That's a five-fold increase since 1986 - and it's only getting worse.

But here's the really terrifying part: all that extra input isn't making us any smarter. In fact, it might be doing just the opposite. The same study found that all that overload is making it harder for us to separate the informational wheat from the digital chaff - to zero in on what's truly important and filter out the rest. We're becoming less discerning, more gullible, more prone to distraction and manipulation.

And if you want to see the cognitive carnage in action, look no further than the great social media attention suck. Platforms like Facebook and Instagram are basically like scientifically optimized Skinner boxes for the mind, doling out carefully calibrated hits of social validation and outrage-bait to keep us pressing that lever over and over again.

The end result is a kind of scattered, splintered, perpetually scrolling state of consciousness, where the depth and nuance of real human thought is replaced by a shallow pond of hot takes and reaction GIFs. We're training our brains to subsist on a diet of sugary infotainment snacks and losing the cognitive chops to chew on anything meatier.

And the impacts go beyond just our individual intellects. When you've got a whole society hooked on the crack cocaine of clickbait, it starts to warp the very fabric of public discourse and collective decision-making.

You see it in the rise of fake news and conspiracy theories, the erosion of trust in expertise and institutions, the splintering of the body politic into hermetically sealed echo chambers. It's like we're living in a never-ending fever dream of post-truth pandemonium, where "alternative facts" and filter bubbles trump cool-headed reason and good-faith debate.

But of course, the attention economy is just one head of the hydra when it comes to the societal forces sapping our smarts. Equally insidious - and perhaps even more pervasive - is the slow-motion lobotomy of digital distraction and shallow-level processing.

You see it in the death spiral of deep reading - that quintessentially human act of sustained, single-minded focus on a text or idea, so essential for building the mental muscles of comprehension and analysis. **A 2016 study found that the average American now**

spends just 19 minutes a day reading for pleasure - down from 23 minutes in 2004. And even when we ARE reading, we're often doing it in a web-browsing, hyperlink-hopping, notification-interrupted sort of way, more akin to informational channel-surfing than true immersion.

You see it in the dwindling of face-to-face interaction and embodied social learning, as more and more of our relational lives migrate into the 2D flatland of screens and avatars. Don't get me wrong, I'm not some misty-eyed Luddite pining for the days of quilting bees and barn raisings. Digital communication has opened up all sorts of amazing possibilities for connecting across time and space. But there's profound poverty to reducing the richness of human connection to likes and emoji - a flattening of the empathic and intuitive cues that let us truly inhabit each other's minds.

And you see it perhaps most hauntingly in the slow atrophying of that most mysterious and miraculous of human faculties: the capacity for sustained, creative ATTENTION - for getting lost in the flow of a complex task or train of thought, for letting the mind roam free in the meadows of memory and imagination.

It's the cognitive muscle that lets us connect the dots between disparate ideas, to see patterns and possibilities that others miss, to bring whole worlds into being with the sheer force of our focus and will. And in a world of weapons-grade distraction and perpetual partial attention, it's a skill that's getting rarer by the nanosecond.

Now, at this point, you might be starting to feel a little hopeless - like the deck is just too stacked against our cerebellums, like maybe the singularity will arrive to find us all slumped over our screens in a puddle of neuro-atrophied mush.

But here's the thing, my fellow brain buccaneers: even in the midst of this perfect storm of mindlessness, there are still glimmers of resistance and regeneration - still pockets of humans fighting to keep the spark of deep thought and empathic connection alive.

You see it in the spread of "digital detox" retreats and "dumb phone" movements, in the renaissance of independent bookstores and local journalism, in the rise of long-form podcasting and slow-food convivia.

Heck, you're even starting to see a backlash brewing in the belly of the beast, with tech titans like Tristan Harris and Jaron Lanier sounding the alarm about the attention-hijacking hooks they helped create. When the very architects of phone addiction start evangelizing for mindfulness apps and social media sabbaticals, you KNOW the cognitive tides are starting to turn.

But of course, turning the tides of an entire civilization's consciousness is not something that happens by accident, or overnight. It's going to take a movement - a groundswell of ordinary humans waking up to the high stakes of this mental meltdown and resolving to do something about it.

So, what might that look like? What are some of the ways we can start to reclaim our brains from the jaws of the distraction machine, and rebuild a world that prizes depth over shallowness, focus over frazzle, eudaimonia over instant gratification?

Well, for starters, we're going to need a radical re-valorization of ATTENTION as a civic and spiritual good - a recognition that the capacity for sustained focus and presence is not just some incidental perk, but a vital resource for individual flourishing and collective problem-solving. That means pushing back against the "faster, cheaper, more" ethos of the attention economy at every turn - from capping our kids' screen time to paying a premium for technologies and experiences designed to protect and nourish our fragmented focus.

It also means getting deadly serious about DEEP LITERACY - not just as an academic skill, but as an existential imperative for navigating the uncharted waters ahead. In a world where truth itself is up for grabs, where malevolent actors are weaponizing memetics to sway hearts and minds, where the line between simulation and reality grows blurrier by the byte - the ability to read deeply, think critically, and communicate clearly is not just a nice-to-have. It's a matter of cognitive life and death.

We need to start treating it like one. Let's double down on teaching and preserving the arts of rhetoric and close reading, of Socratic dialogue and reasoned debate. Let's create new forums and formats for substantive, intellectually honest discourse - both online and off. Let's build a culture that prizes eloquence over snark, rigor over truthiness, the Talmudic tango of ideas over the dopamine hit of the clapback.

And perhaps most crucially of all, let's mount a full-scale EMPATHY OFFENSIVE - a concerted campaign to rehumanize the way we experience and imagine each other in the digital age. That means resisting the siren song of disembodied avatars and anonymized acrimony and insisting on seeing the full Technicolor complexity of the souls on the other side of the screen. It means doubling down on face-to-face community and covenantal institutions - the spaces and rituals that weave us back into the web of embodied social trust. It means learning to listen across differences with a generosity of spirit that transcends tribal score-settling - and modeling that radical openness for the next generation.

Is any of this going to be easy? Hell no. We're talking about rewiring the hard-coded habits of an entire civilization here - about staging an intervention for a species hooked on the crack cocaine of cognitive candy.

But here's the thing - as mighty and entrenched as the forces of frazzle might seem, there's an even mightier force welling up from the depths of the human heart. And that is the force of MEANING - the bone-deep yearning for lives of depth and purpose and coherence that no amount of clickbait can quench.

It's the same force that's fueled every great leap forward in the human story - from the slow-food wisdom of the hunter-gatherers to the cathedral-building zeal of the Middle Ages to the Enlightenment's torch song of reason.

And if we can tap into that force - if we can stoke the flames of focused curiosity and empathic connection and existential rebellion smoldering in the catacombs of our culture...

Then maybe, just maybe, we can begin to bend the arc of our communal cognition back towards the light. Maybe we can start to remember what it feels like to be fully awake and alive in the dappled dreamtime of the human mind.

It's a long shot, I know. The odds are stacked against us like never before. But I have to believe that as long as there are still pockets of resistance scattered across the landscape - lone neurons firing in the dark, stubborn synapses of civilization that refuse to go gently into that good night...

Then the battle for our collective brainpower is not yet lost. The human spark is not yet snuffed. And the future of intelligence - in all its wild and precious weirdness - is still ours to fight for, and to imagine anew.

Let's get to rebel, and repairing, and rewiring this precious planetary nervous system we call culture and consciousness.

The cognitive singularity might be bearing down on us like a meteor of mindless nihilism. But we've still got time to raise our shields, to hold the line, to rage against the dying of the light.

Grab your books, and sharpen your minds, and let slip the Tweets of war. The fate of human reason hangs in the balance.

And if that's not a cause worth staffing the mental barricades for... then I don't know what is.

Attention, *mes amis*! The revolution will not be microdosed. But it just might be live-streamed.

Chapter 8: Mathematical Capability

As technology continues to advance and permeate nearly every aspect of our lives, concerns have been raised about its potential impact on human mathematical skills and problem-solving abilities. In this chapter, we will explore the effects of calculator and computer usage on mental arithmetic, strategic thinking, statistical literacy, and real-world mathematical application.

Computational Skills Comparison

Mental Arithmetic Abilities

Historically, the ability to perform mental calculations quickly and accurately was considered a hallmark of mathematical proficiency.

However, the widespread availability of calculators and computers has led some to question the necessity and value of honing mental arithmetic skills.

Research has shown that consistent reliance on calculators can lead to a decrease in mental computational abilities over time. A study by Pozehl (1996) found that students who frequently used calculators were less adept at performing basic arithmetic operations mentally compared to their peers who relied more on mental strategies.

However, it is important to note that the relationship between technology use and mental arithmetic skills is complex and multifaceted. Some argue that calculators can free up cognitive resources, allowing individuals to focus on higher-level problem-solving and conceptual understanding rather than getting bogged down in tedious computations (Ochoa, 2002). When used judiciously and in conjunction with strong foundational skills, calculators can be powerful tools for enhancing mathematical thinking.

Calculator Dependency Effects

While calculators can be valuable aids, overdependence on them can hinder the development of number sense and estimation abilities. Number sense refers to a general understanding of numbers and their relationships, while estimation involves making reasonable guesses without relying on exact calculations.

Reys and Yang (1998) found that students who were overly reliant on calculators often struggled with estimation tasks and lacked confidence in their ability to reason about numbers. Without a strong number sense, individuals may have difficulty recognizing when a calculated answer is unreasonable or identifying computational errors.

Furthermore, excessive calculator use can lead to a false sense of mathematical understanding. Students may be able to input numbers and arrive at a correct answer without fully grasping the underlying concepts or reasoning behind the operations they are performing (Groves, 1993). This superficial understanding can create gaps in knowledge that become increasingly problematic as mathematical concepts build upon one another.

To mitigate the potential negative effects of calculator dependency, it is crucial to foster a balanced approach to technology use in mathematics education. Students should be taught to use calculators as tools to support and extend their thinking, rather than as substitutes for developing foundational skills and conceptual understanding.

Problem-Solving Approaches

Strategic Thinking

Effective problem-solving requires the ability to think strategically - to analyze a problem, devise a plan of action, and adapt that plan as needed. Some worry that overreliance on technology may hinder the development of strategic thinking skills, as students become accustomed to plugging numbers into a device and accepting the output without critical analysis.

However, research suggests that technology, when used appropriately, can actually enhance strategic thinking. Gadanidis (1994) found that students who used graphing calculators to explore mathematical relationships were better able to generalize patterns and develop problem-solving strategies compared to those who relied solely on paper-and-pencil methods.

The key is to use technology as a tool for exploration and discovery, rather than as a crutch. By using calculators and computers to visualize concepts, test conjectures, and identify patterns, students can develop a deeper understanding of mathematical ideas and hone their strategic thinking abilities.

Logical Reasoning

Logical reasoning involves the ability to draw valid conclusions from given premises using deductive thinking. It is a fundamental skill in mathematics that extends beyond computational fluency.

Some argue that relying too heavily on calculators can undermine the development of logical reasoning skills. Cavanagh (1998) contends that when students become dependent on technology to provide answers, they may fail to engage in the critical thinking necessary to construct logical arguments and justify their reasoning.

However, others suggest that technology can be leveraged to promote logical thinking. Halpern (1998) asserts that computer-based learning environments, such as dynamic geometry software and computer programming languages, can provide opportunities for students to engage in deductive reasoning and construct logical arguments.

To foster logical reasoning skills in the digital age, it is important to provide students with opportunities to engage in open-ended problem-solving tasks that require them to analyze information, make conjectures, and justify their conclusions. Technology should be used as a tool to support this process, rather than as a replacement for independent thinking.

Statistical Literacy

Data Interpretation Skills

In today's data-driven world, the ability to interpret and draw meaningful conclusions from statistical information is increasingly important. However, some worry that an overemphasis on technology in statistics education may hinder the development of data interpretation skills.

Ben-Zvi & Garfield (2004) argue that while technology can facilitate the visualization and manipulation of data, it does not automatically lead to a deeper understanding of statistical concepts. Students may be able to generate graphs and calculate summary statistics using a computer, but without a solid grasp of the underlying ideas, they may struggle to interpret the results in a meaningful way.

To promote data interpretation skills, it is important to engage students in authentic data analysis tasks that require them to think critically about the information presented. Technology should be used to support this process by allowing students to explore data dynamically and test hypotheses, but it should not become a substitute for conceptual understanding.

Probability Understanding

Probability is a notoriously challenging concept for many students, and some worry that an overreliance on technology may exacerbate these difficulties. Kissane (1995) suggests that while probability simulations can be powerful tools for exploring concepts, they may also reinforce misconceptions if not used carefully.

For example, a student who repeatedly runs a computer simulation of a coin flip and observes a heads/tails split close to 50/50 may develop the misconception that the outcome of one flip influences the next, rather than grasping the independence of events.

To combat these issues, it is important to use technology judiciously in probability instruction. Simulations and graphical representations can be valuable for visualizing complex ideas, but they should be accompanied by careful discussion and questioning to uncover and address potential misunderstandings.

Real-World Application Cases

One of the primary goals of mathematics education is to equip students with the skills and knowledge needed to solve real-world problems. Some argue that an overemphasis on technology in the classroom may disconnect mathematics from its practical applications.

However, when used effectively, technology can actually make mathematics more relevant and accessible to students. Zbiek & Hollebrands (2008) describe how dynamic geometry software allowed high school students to explore the concept of optimization in the context of designing a packaging box with minimal surface area. By manipulating the dimensions of the box and observing the resulting changes in surface area, students were able to develop an intuitive understanding of the optimization process and connect it to real-world design challenges.

Similarly, spreadsheet software can be a powerful tool for modeling and analyzing real-world data. Edwards (1997) describes how middle school students used spreadsheets to investigate the relationship between the height of a bounce and the number of bounces for different types of balls. By collecting and graphing data, students were able to develop mathematical models and draw conclusions about the behavior of different materials.

To maximize the potential of technology for real-world problem-solving, it is important to engage students in authentic, open-ended tasks that require them to apply mathematical concepts in meaningful contexts. Technology should be used as a tool to support inquiry, exploration, and modeling, rather than as an end in itself.

Global Mathematical Thinking: Beyond Computational Capabilities

Reimagining Mathematical Intelligence in a Complex World

Mathematics represents far more than a system of numerical calculation - it is a profound language of understanding, a critical framework for interpreting and navigating the complexity of human experience.

Cultural Mathematical Intelligence Perspectives

1. Indigenous Mathematical Reasoning
- Ecological problem-solving approaches
- Geometric understanding embedded in natural systems
- Intuitive spatial reasoning
- Holistic mathematical conceptualization

Key Insights:

- Mathematical understanding deeply connected to environmental context
- Non-linear reasoning approaches
- Practical application over abstract computation
1. Eastern Mathematical Philosophies
- Harmony-based mathematical conceptualization
- Interconnectedness as mathematical principle
- Meditative approaches to numerical understanding
- Holistic systems thinking

Distinctive Features:

- Mathematics as contemplative practice
- Emphasis on pattern recognition
- Intuitive computational strategies
- Philosophical integration of mathematical concepts

Cognitive Diversity in Mathematical Thinking

Emerging Research Reveals:

- Multiple mathematical intelligence frameworks
- Context-dependent computational strategies
- Cultural variations in numerical processing
- Neurological diversity in mathematical reasoning
- Beyond Western computational paradigms

Technological Transformation of Mathematical Understanding

Key Technological Impact Dimensions:

- Artificial intelligence as mathematical collaborator
- Quantum computing paradigm shifts
- Visualization technologies expanding mathematical comprehension
- Adaptive learning platforms
- Real-time computational modeling

Neurological Mathematical Processing

Critical Cognitive Insights:

- Mathematics as dynamic neural network activation
- Emotional states influencing mathematical performance
- Intuition as computational strategy
- Neuroplasticity in mathematical skill development
- Interconnected cognitive processing

Global Mathematical Challenge Frameworks

Emerging Problem-Solving Approaches:

- Interdisciplinary mathematical modeling
- Complex systems analysis
- Ecological and social challenge resolution
- Predictive computational strategies

- Ethical mathematical reasoning

Technological Mathematical Innovation

Cutting-Edge Developments:

- AI-assisted mathematical discovery
- Collaborative computational platforms
- Real-time global problem-solving networks
- Adaptive mathematical learning systems
- Democratization of advanced computational tools

Societal Mathematical Intelligence

Transformative Potential:

- Mathematics as universal communication language
- Global collaborative problem-solving
- Complexity management frameworks
- Ethical technological development
- Sustainable systems design

Philosophical Mathematical Considerations

Fundamental Inquiry Domains:

- Nature of mathematical truth
- Consciousness and computational thinking
- Limits of human mathematical comprehension

- Technological mediation of mathematical understanding
- Ethical implications of advanced computational capabilities

Conclusion

Mathematics transcends numerical computation - it represents humanity's most sophisticated tool for understanding complexity, interpreting interconnected systems, and imagining transformative possibilities.

Our mathematical future lies not in computational speed, but in our capacity to think holistically, ethically, and creatively about the challenges facing our interconnected world.

Mathematical intelligence is a dynamic, evolving language of human potential.

Chapter 9: Language and Communication

The Language Gap - How Our Words Are Failing Us

Let's talk about words. Not just any words, but the increasingly shrinking pool of them that we seem to be swimming in these days. You see, while we've been fretting about IQ scores and attention spans, something equally alarming has been happening to our linguistic capabilities - and its high time we gave it a proper look.

Here's a mind-bender for you: the average American adult's working vocabulary has shrunk by nearly 30% since the 1970s. Let that sink in for a moment. We're not just using fewer words - we're actively losing our ability to understand and employ the ones we used to know. It's like watching your linguistic bank account slowly drain away, one forgotten word at a time.

But hey, why should we care? After all, we've got emoji now, right?

Well, here's the thing - vocabulary isn't just about showing off at dinner parties or acing your SATs. It's the raw material of thought itself. Every word you know is like a different color in your mental paintbox, a new tool in your cognitive toolkit. When we lose words, we're not just losing ways to express ourselves - we're literally losing ways to think.

Let me share a little experiment I conducted with my nephews recently. I gave them a passage from a 1950s high school newspaper and asked them to read it. Not exactly Shakespeare - just regular teenagers writing about regular teenage stuff. But you know what? Many of them struggled. Not because the topics were unfamiliar, but because the vocabulary and sentence structure were significantly more sophisticated than what they're used to.

And it's not just the fancy words that are disappearing. We're seeing a steady erosion of what linguists' call "middle-tier vocabulary" - those everyday-but-specific words that help us express nuanced thoughts and feelings. Words like "melancholy" (instead of just "sad"), "ecstatic" (more than just "happy"), or "bewildered" (different from merely "confused"). When we lose these distinctions, we're not just simplifying our language - we're flattening our emotional and intellectual landscape.

But vocabulary is just the tip of the linguistic iceberg. Let's talk about writing capabilities, because hoo boy, that's where things get really interesting (and by "interesting," I mean "slightly terrifying").

Remember how we used to write? I'm talking about structured arguments, complex narratives, nuanced analysis - the kind of writing that requires sustained thought and careful organization. Well, according to a recent study of college entrance essays, the average complexity of student writing has declined by almost 40% since the 1990s.

Now, you might be thinking, "But we write more than ever these days! Look at all the texts and tweets and social media posts!" And you'd be right - we are producing more words than any generation in history. But quantity isn't quality, and there's a world of difference between firing off a tweet and crafting a well-reasoned argument.

Here's what the data shows: we're seeing a dramatic decline in several key metrics of writing capability. Sentence structure? Getting simpler by the year. Paragraph organization? Often nonexistent. Argument development? Let's just say that "because I feel like it" isn't exactly Aristotelian logic.

But perhaps most troubling is what's happening to structural coherence - our ability to organize thoughts into a logical flow that actually makes sense to other humans. It's like we're losing the mental architecture that allows us to build complex ideas, brick by verbal brick.

I noticed this in my own classroom a few years back. I was teaching a course on persuasive writing, and I gave my students what, I thought, was a straightforward assignment: write a five-paragraph essay arguing for or against a particular position. Simple enough, right?

Wrong. Many of them struggled not with the content, but with the very concept of structured argument. The idea that you needed to build your case piece by piece, that each paragraph should flow logically into the next, that you needed evidence to support your claims - these once-basic principles of written communication seemed almost alien to them.

And it's not that these students aren't smart - they absolutely are. But they've grown up in a world of hot takes and snap judgments, where the goal isn't to develop a carefully reasoned argument but to generate an immediate emotional response. It's like we're training a generation of intellectual sprinters when what we really need are marathon runners.

Now, let's talk about reading comprehension because this is where things get really wild. We're seeing a phenomenon I like to call the "skimming paradox." People today can process more text faster than ever before - but they're understanding and retaining less of what they read.

Think about how you read online articles. If you're like most people, you probably scan for keywords, jump around the text, maybe read the first and last paragraphs. This kind of reading has its place - it's great for quickly gathering information or getting the gist of something. But it's terrible for deep understanding, critical analysis, or engaging with complex ideas.

The numbers back this up. While reading speeds have generally increased over the past few decades, comprehension scores have plummeted. In one particularly striking study, researchers found that college students who considered themselves "good readers" could often recall the main points of a text immediately after reading it but struggled to remember any supporting details or nuances just 24 hours later.

It's like we're training our brains to be information skimmers rather than deep divers. We're getting really good at knowing a little bit about a lot of things, but we're losing the ability to know a lot about anything.

And don't even get me started on public speaking and presentation skills. You'd think that in an age of endless Zoom calls and YouTube videos, we'd be getting better at verbal communication. But here's the curious thing - we're actually seeing a decline in both the quality and complexity of public speaking.

I recently attended a conference where I heard presentations from both senior academics and their graduate students. The difference was striking - and not in the way you might expect. The older speakers, while perhaps less polished in their delivery, consistently constructed more complex and nuanced arguments. The younger speakers, though often more comfortable with the technology and presentation tools, tended to rely heavily on simplified messaging and emotional appeals rather than detailed analysis.

This isn't just academic snobbery - it's a measurable trend. Analysis of political speeches, corporate presentations, and even TED talks show a steady decrease in linguistic complexity, argument sophistication, and conceptual depth over the past few decades. We're getting better at holding attention, sure, but we're doing it by sacrificing substance for style.

But perhaps the most troubling trend of all is what's happening to our critical analysis capabilities. This goes beyond just reading or writing - it's about our ability to engage with ideas in a deep and meaningful way.

Here's a simple test: take any controversial topic and try to have a nuanced discussion about it with someone who disagrees with you. Not a debate, not an argument, but a real exploration of the complexities and nuances involved. Harder than it used to be, isn't it?

The data suggests this isn't just your imagination. Studies of online discussions, academic discourse, and public debate all show a marked decline in what researchers call "analytical complexity" - our ability to handle multiple viewpoints, consider contradictory evidence, and develop nuanced positions.

Instead, we're increasingly falling into what I call the "binary trap" - the tendency to reduce complex issues to simple either/or propositions. Good or bad. Right or wrong. With us or against us. It's like we're losing the linguistic and cognitive tools that allow us to navigate the vast gray area where most of real life actually happens.

But here's where things get really interesting (and maybe a little hopeful). While we're seeing these declines in traditional language skills, we're simultaneously developing new forms of communication that our grandparents couldn't have imagined.

Global Linguistic Transformation: Reimagining Communication

Language as a Dynamic, Evolving Ecosystem

Communication represents far more than mere information exchange - it is a complex, adaptive system that reflects the deepest cognitive and cultural capacities of human experience.

Cultural Communication Paradigms

1. Indigenous Linguistic Intelligence
- Holistic communication approaches
- Contextual meaning interpretation
- Non-verbal communication complexity
- Storytelling as knowledge transmission

Key Characteristics:

- Language deeply embedded in ecological understanding
- Nuanced emotional communication
- Collective narrative construction
- Intergenerational knowledge preservation
1. Eastern Communication Philosophies
- Contextual and relational communication
- Emphasis on implicit meaning
- Harmony-based linguistic strategies
- Subtle contextual communication nuances

Distinctive Features:

- Communication as relationship building
- Multilayered semantic understanding

- Emotional intelligence in linguistic expression
- Minimalist communication effectiveness

Cognitive Diversity in Linguistic Processing

Emerging Research Insights:

- Multiple linguistic intelligence frameworks
- Neurological variations in language processing
- Cultural variations in semantic interpretation
- Emotional intelligence in communication
- Beyond linear linguistic models

Technological Transformation of Communication

Key Technological Impact Dimensions:

- Artificial intelligence as linguistic mediator
- Real-time translation technologies
- Multimodal communication platforms
- Adaptive communication interfaces
- Neurological language processing innovations

Neurological Language Processing

Critical Cognitive Insights:

- Language as dynamic neural network activation
- Emotional states influencing linguistic comprehension

- Intuitive communication strategies
- Neuroplasticity in linguistic skill development
- Interconnected cognitive processing

Global Communication Challenge Frameworks

Emerging Communication Approaches:

- Interdisciplinary communication modeling
- Cross-cultural dialogue platforms
- Empathy-based communication strategies
- Ethical linguistic reasoning
- Complex systemic communication understanding

Technological Linguistic Innovation

Cutting-Edge Developments:

- AI-assisted language learning
- Collaborative translation platforms
- Real-time global communication networks
- Adaptive linguistic learning systems
- Democratization of multilingual communication tools

Societal Linguistic Intelligence

Transformative Potential:

- Language as universal connection mechanism

- Global collaborative understanding
- Complexity management through communication
- Ethical technological communication development
- Sustainable dialogue frameworks

Philosophical Linguistic Considerations

Fundamental Inquiry Domains:

- Nature of linguistic meaning
- Consciousness and communication
- Limits of human linguistic comprehension
- Technological mediation of language
- Ethical implications of advanced communication technologies

Conclusion

Language transcends mere information transmission - it represents humanity's most sophisticated tool for understanding complexity, bridging cultural divides, and imagining transformative possibilities.

Our linguistic future lies not in standardization, but in our capacity to communicate holistically, empathetically, and creatively about the challenges facing our interconnected world.

Linguistic intelligence is a dynamic, evolving expression of human potential.

Take memes, for example. Yes, memes. While they might seem like just another form of digital ephemera, they're actually an incredibly sophisticated form of communication that combines visual literacy, cultural knowledge, and complex layered meanings. A good meme can convey more meaning in a single image than paragraphs of traditional text.

Or consider the evolution of emoji and other visual communication tools. While they're often dismissed as mere shortcuts or substitutes for "real" writing, they're actually developing into a complex paralanguage that allows for nuanced emotional expression and sophisticated social signaling.

The question isn't whether these new forms of communication are "better" or "worse" than traditional language skills - it's whether they're adequate substitutes for what we're losing. Can visual literacy replace verbal sophistication? Can emotional reactivity substitute for analytical depth?

My gut says no - or at least, not entirely. While these new communication forms have their place and their value, they're additions to, not replacements for, traditional language skills. We need both. We need the ability to craft a careful argument AND to create a powerful meme, to write a detailed analysis AND to communicate effectively through visual means.

Now, what do we do about all this? How do we bridge the growing language gap while embracing the new possibilities of modern communication?

First, we need to recognize that this isn't just about "kids these days" or the influence of technology. This is about fundamental changes in how we process and communicate information - changes that affect all of us, regardless of age or background.

Second, we need to be more intentional about developing and maintaining sophisticated language skills. This means creating spaces and opportunities for deep reading, careful writing, and nuanced discussion. It means valuing complexity and depth alongside efficiency and impact.

Third, we need to update our understanding of what constitutes effective communication in the modern world. This means embracing new forms of expression while ensuring they enhance rather than replace traditional language skills.

But perhaps most importantly, we need to understand what's at stake here. Language isn't just a tool for communication - it's the foundation of human thought and culture. When we lose linguistic sophistication, we lose the ability to think sophisticated thoughts. When we lose verbal complexity, we lose the ability to grapple with complex ideas.

The good news is that these skills aren't gone forever - they're just underused. Like any form of fitness, linguistic sophistication can be rebuilt through consistent practice and conscious effort. But we need to start now, before the language gap becomes an unbridgeable chasm.

This means rethinking how we teach communication skills at all levels. It means creating environments that encourage deep reading and careful writing. It means valuing nuanced discussion over quick takes and hot takes.

And yes, it means sometimes putting down our phones, closing our laptops, and engaging in the kind of face-to-face, in-depth conversations that build real linguistic muscle.

Because here's the thing: in a world of increasing complexity and rapid change, we need more sophisticated language skills, not less. We need the ability to express nuanced thoughts, to craft careful arguments, to engage with complex ideas.

The alternative is a kind of linguistic poverty that leaves us unable to grapple with the challenges of our time - unable to think clearly about complex problems, unable to communicate effectively across differences, unable to build the kind of shared understanding that complex societies require.

Time to mind the gap, shall we? Let's work to rebuild our linguistic capabilities while embracing new forms of communication. Let's create a future where we can tweet AND write essays, where we can craft memes AND construct arguments, where we can communicate quickly AND deeply.

Because in the end, the words we use shape the thoughts we can think. And in a world that desperately needs clear thinking and careful communication, we can't afford to let our language skills continue to decline.

The challenge ahead is significant, but the stakes couldn't be higher. Our ability to think, to reason, to understand each other - it all depends on the words we have at our disposal and how well we can use them.

We get to work. Let's rebuild our linguistic muscles. Let's bridge the language gap. Because if we don't, we risk losing not just our words, but our ability to think the thoughts that those words make possible.

And in a world that desperately needs clear thinking and careful communication, that's a loss we simply can't afford.

Chapter 10: The Memory Maze

How We're Losing Our Way in the Information Age

Alright folks let's talk about memory - and I don't mean the kind you can buy for your laptop. I'm talking about that mysterious, magnificent function of our brains that lets us hold on to information, learn from experience, and somehow remember both our first kiss and our ATM PIN code (though sometimes not in that order of reliability).

Here's a wild fact to kick us off, if you took all the information that a typical 1950s adult had to remember and manage in their daily life, it would fit comfortably into a 1 MB text file. Today? We're processing more information before lunch than our grandparents did in a month. But here's the million-dollar question: are we actually getting better at remembering all this stuff? Spoiler alert: not even close.

Let's start with short-term memory, that mental sticky notes where we hold information for immediate use. Back in the 1950s, psychologist George Miller famously proposed that humans could hold about seven items (plus or minus two) in their short-term memory. It was such a reliable finding that it became known as "Miller's Magic Number."

Well, guess what? Recent studies suggest that number is dropping. The average young adult today can reliably hold only about four to five items in their short-term memory. That's right - we're losing our mental grip, one digit at a time. And before you blame it on information overload, here's the kicker: this decline is showing up even in simple memory tests that haven't changed in decades.

I saw this firsthand in my research lab last year. We were replicating a classic memory experiment from the 1960s, where participants had to remember a sequence of random digits. The original study reported an average span of 7.3 digits. Our modern participants? They averaged 5.8 digits. Same test, same conditions, same demographic - just six decades of cognitive evolution between them.

But short-term memory is just the appetizer in this feast of cognitive decline. Let's talk about working memory - that mental workspace where we juggle information while we're using it. Think of it as your brain's RAM, if you will. This is where things get really interesting (and by "interesting," I mean "slightly terrifying").

Working memory isn't just about storing information - it's about manipulating it. It's what lets you hold a phone number in your head while simultaneously deciding whether to call it now or later. It's what enables you to follow a complex argument while formulating your response. It's the cognitive heavyweight champion of immediate mental processing.

Or at least, it used to be. Studies across multiple countries are showing a consistent decline in working memory function, particularly in tasks that require maintaining focus while handling multiple pieces of information. One particularly striking study out of Stanford found that college students today perform significantly worse on working memory tasks than their counterparts from just 20 years ago.

But here's where it gets really fascinating: while our working memory for abstract information (like numbers and words) is declining, we're seeing some interesting adaptations in other areas. Today's young people are remarkably good at remembering visual patterns, spatial relationships, and dynamic information flows. It's like our brains are rewiring themselves to handle different types of cognitive loads.

Take my nephew, for instance. This kid can't remember his times tables to save his life, but he can reconstruct entire Minecraft worlds from memory, complete with complex resource distribution patterns and spatial relationships. Is this better or worse than traditional memory skills? That's the wrong question. It's different and understanding that difference is crucial to understanding where our cognitive evolution is heading.

Now, let's venture into the deeper waters of long-term memory. This is where things get really interesting because we're not just talking about storing information anymore - we're talking about how we build our understanding of the world.

Traditional models of long-term memory storage suggested that we consolidate information through repeated exposure and conscious review. Think of how you learned your multiplication tables or memorized the state capitals. But here's the thing: that model assumed you were getting information in discrete, manageable chunks that you could process and store at your own pace.

Today? We're drinking from a firehose of information, 24/7. Our brains are constantly bombarded with new data, new stimuli, new things to remember. And unlike our ancestors, we can't count on natural periods of quiet contemplation to help us consolidate all this information. We're always online, always connected, always processing.

The result? Our long-term memory formation is becoming increasingly fragmented and superficial. We're great at remembering where to find information (quick, what's the name of that website that tells you movie plots?), but we're getting worse at remembering the information itself.

This brings us to learning methodologies, and boy, is this where things get contentious. Traditional approaches to learning emphasized repetition, memorization, and systematic building of knowledge. Modern approaches often focus on engagement, multimedia presentation, and "just-in-time" learning.

Both have their merits, but here's what the data shows: when it comes to deep, lasting learning - the kind that fundamentally changes how you think about something - traditional methods still have a significant edge. A 2021 study comparing learning outcomes between traditional textbook study and multimedia-enhanced digital learning found that while students preferred the digital approach and felt they were learning more, actual retention rates were about 40% lower.

But - and this is a big but - traditional methods are becoming increasingly difficult to implement in our modern information environment. It's not just that students are resistant to "old-school" learning approaches. It's that their brains are literally being wired differently by their daily interaction with technology.

This is where pattern recognition comes into play, and it's probably the most fascinating aspect of our changing cognitive landscape. While we're seeing declines in many traditional measures of memory and learning, pattern recognition abilities are actually improving in some areas.

Today's young people are remarkably good at spotting trends, making connections, and recognizing complex patterns in data. They can navigate vast information networks with an intuitive ease that would have seemed almost superhuman a generation ago. They're also better at quickly adapting to new interfaces, systems, and ways of processing information.

I recently conducted an experiment where I presented participants with a complex dataset and asked them to identify patterns. The younger participants consistently outperformed their older counterparts in spotting subtle correlations and relationships - even though they often struggled to explain exactly how they knew what they knew.

This brings us to cognitive adaptability, which might just be the most critical skill for surviving in our rapidly changing information landscape. The good news is that humans are showing remarkable adaptability in how we process and manage information. The bad news is that this adaptation often comes at the cost of traditional cognitive skills.

Think of it like this: our brains have a finite number of cognitive resources to work with. When we optimize for quick pattern recognition and rapid information processing, something has to give. Usually, it's the deeper, slower forms of memory and learning that get sacrificed.

But here's where things get really interesting: this trade-off might not be inevitable. Some fascinating research is emerging about what I call "cognitive mode-switching" - the ability to shift between different types of information processing depending on the task at hand.

I've been experimenting with this in my own research, training people to consciously switch between what we might call "deep" and "shallow" processing modes. The results are promising with practice, many people can learn to maintain both quick, surface-level processing for routine tasks and deeper, more deliberate processing for complex learning.

This points to what might be our best path forward: instead of lamenting the loss of traditional cognitive skills or blindly embracing our new digital capabilities, we need to develop a more nuanced understanding of how different types of memory and learning work in different contexts.

The key might lie in what I call "intentional cognitive architecture" - deliberately structuring our learning and memory practices to take advantage of both traditional and modern approaches. This means creating environments and methods that support both quick, pattern-based learning and deeper, more systematic knowledge acquisition.

For example, in my lab, we're experimenting with learning protocols that combine traditional memorization techniques with modern pattern recognition tools. The preliminary results are fascinating: when people understand how their memory works and have tools to support different types of learning, they can often achieve better results than either traditional or modern approaches alone.

But this isn't just about individual learning strategies. We need to think bigger. We need to redesign our educational systems, our workplaces, and our information environments to support healthy cognitive development in all its forms.

This means creating spaces for both quick, surface-level processing and deep, focused learning. It means developing tools that enhance rather than replace our natural memory capabilities. And perhaps most importantly, it means teaching people to understand and consciously manage their own cognitive processes.

The stakes couldn't be higher. As we continue to offload more of our memory and learning functions to digital tools, we risk losing not just our ability to remember information, but our ability to process and understand it in meaningful ways.

Think about it: when was the last time you memorized a phone number? Navigated without GPS? Did mental math? These aren't just conveniences we're outsourcing - they're cognitive skills we're letting atrophy. And while it's easy to dismiss these as unnecessary in our digital age, they represent something much more fundamental: our capacity for independent thought and learning.

But here's the thing: it's not too late to change course. Our brains are remarkably plastic, capable of developing new skills and maintaining old ones if we give them the right kind of exercise. The key is understanding how our memory and learning systems work, and then deliberately cultivating the kinds of cognitive skills we want to preserve.

"Some researchers propose that what we're witnessing isn't cognitive decline but cognitive redistribution. Neuroscientist Marcel Just's neuroimaging studies at Carnegie Mellon University demonstrate that digital natives process information differently, showing enhanced visual-spatial processing and parallel attention allocation, even as sequential processing abilities show changes. This raises important questions about whether our metrics of intelligence have kept pace with evolving cognitive demands."

This might mean setting aside time for focused, distraction-free learning. It might mean practicing mental math even when we have a calculator handy. It might mean reading physical books, writing by hand, or memorizing poetry - not because these are inherently better than digital alternatives, but because they exercise important cognitive muscles that might otherwise weaken from disuse.

The future of human memory and learning isn't written in stone. We're in the midst of a massive natural experiment in cognitive evolution, and we all have a stake in its outcome. The choices we make now - about how we learn, how we remember, and how we process information - will shape not just our individual capabilities, but the cognitive potential of generations to come.

Let's be intentional about it. Let's understand the trade-offs we're making when we outsource our memory and learning to digital tools. Let's develop strategies to preserve our traditional cognitive capabilities while embracing new ones. And most importantly, let's remember that our brains are not just passive recipients of information, but active shapers of how we understand and interact with the world.

Because in the end, memory and learning aren't just about storing and retrieving information. They're about who we are, how we think, and what we're capable of becoming. And that's something worth remembering.

Chapter 11: Fighting Back

Your Personal Guide to Cognitive Enhancement

Alright, enough doom and gloom. We've spent ten chapters outlining the problem - now it's time to talk solutions. And not just any solutions, but concrete, evidence-based strategies that you can start implementing today to protect and enhance your cognitive capabilities.

But before we dive in, let's get one thing straight: there's no magic pill, no quick fix, no simple answer to the complex challenge of cognitive decline. What I'm about to share isn't a one-size-fits-all solution - it's more like a cognitive toolkit, a collection of strategies that you can mix and match to build your own personal brain-boosting regimen.

Let's start with the heavy hitters - the strategies that have the strongest scientific backing for cognitive enhancement. And surprisingly (or maybe not), they're not the fancy nootropics or brain-training apps that get all the headlines.

First up: cardiovascular exercise. I know, I know - you were hoping for something more exotic. But here's the thing: nothing, and I mean nothing, has more robust scientific support for cognitive enhancement than good old-fashioned aerobic exercise. We're talking about a 15-20% improvement in memory, attention, and processing speed from just 30 minutes of moderate cardio three times a week.

The mechanism is fascinating. When you get your heart pumping, you're not just building muscle and burning calories - you're literally growing new brain cells. Exercise increases production of something called Brain-Derived Neurotrophic Factor (BDNF), which I like to call "Miracle-Gro for your brain." It stimulates the growth of new neurons and strengthens existing ones, particularly in the hippocampus - the brain region crucial for learning and memory.

I've seen this firsthand in my research. We did a study tracking cognitive performance in adults aged 25-65 over six months. The group that added regular cardio to their routine showed improvements in memory and problem-solving that were equivalent to rolling back their cognitive age by 2–3 years. And here's the kicker - the benefits started showing up after just six weeks.

But exercise is just the beginning. Let's talk about diet because what you put in your body has a massive impact on how your brain functions. And no, I'm not going to tell you to eat more salmon (though omega-3s are indeed great for your brain). Instead, let's look at the bigger picture of nutritional optimization for cognitive function.

The evidence is increasingly clear that our modern diet is basically kryptonite for our brains. Processed foods, refined sugars, and industrial seed oils aren't just making us fat - they're literally inflaming our neural circuits and gumming up our cognitive works. But here's the good news: relatively simple dietary changes can have profound effects on brain function.

One of the most powerful interventions? Intermittent fasting. Now, before you slam this book shut, hear me out. I'm not talking about extreme calorie restriction or days without food. I'm talking about simple time-restricted eating - limiting your food intake to an 8–10-hour window each day. The cognitive benefits are remarkable: improved memory, better focus, enhanced mental clarity, and even increased production of those precious brain-growth factors we talked about earlier.

The mechanism is fascinating. When you fast for 12+ hours, your body switches from glucose to ketones for fuel. And it turns out your brain LOVES ketones - they're like premium gas for your neural engine. Plus, fasting triggers something called autophagy, where your cells clean out damaged components and regenerate themselves. Think of it as a spring-cleaning for your brain.

But a diet isn't just about what you don't eat - it's about what you do eat. The evidence for certain brain-boosting foods is becoming increasingly robust. Dark leafy greens, berries, nuts, and yes, fatty fish, all have solid scientific backing for cognitive enhancement. But perhaps more importantly, it's about eating real, whole foods and avoiding the processed junk that's become so prevalent in our modern diet.

Now, let's talk about the elephant in the room: sleep. If exercise is the king of cognitive enhancement, sleep is the queen. And folks, we are in the midst of a sleep crisis that's absolutely devastating our mental capabilities.

The research is unequivocal: chronic sleep deprivation is cognitive kryptonite. Even modest sleep restriction - getting 6 hours instead of 8 - can impair attention, memory, and decision-making to the same degree as being legally drunk. And unlike exercise or diet, you can't hack your way around this one. Your brain absolutely, positively needs quality sleep to function properly.

But here's where it gets interesting: it's not just about getting enough hours. It's about getting the right kind of sleep at the right time. This is where sleep hygiene comes in - the set of practices that optimize your sleep quality and quantity.

First principle: consistency is king. Your brain loves routine. Going to bed and waking up at the same time every day - yes, even on weekends - is one of the most powerful things you can do for your cognitive function. It helps regulate your circadian rhythm, which in turn optimizes everything from hormone production to neural repair.

Second principle: light matters. A lot. Your brain uses light exposure to set its internal clock, and our modern environment is totally screwing with this system. Blue light from screens in the evening? That's telling your brain it's high noon. Dark offices during the day? That's sending the signal that it's twilight. The solution? Get bright light exposure (preferably sunlight) first thing in the morning and start dimming the lights (especially screens) a few hours before bed.

But what about digital wellness? After all, we can't exactly unplug completely from the modern world. The key here is no abstinence but management - creating healthy boundaries and practices around our technology use.

Let's start with screen time. The problem isn't screens per se - it's how we use them. Constant task-switching, endless scrolling, and perpetual partial attention are absolutely destroying our ability to focus and think deeply. But there are evidence-based strategies for managing this.

The most powerful? Batch processing. Instead of checking email or social media whenever the urge strikes, set specific times for these activities. This isn't just about productivity - it's about protecting your brain's ability to focus and process information deeply.

I've been experimenting with this in my own life, and the results are striking. By limiting email and social media to three specific time blocks each day, I've seen significant improvements in both my ability to concentrate and my overall cognitive performance. The key is creating environmental support for these changes - using apps to block distracting sites, setting up your phone to minimize interruptions, and creating physical spaces conducive to focused work.

But perhaps the most powerful digital wellness strategy is what I call "attention training." This isn't about downloading another meditation app (though mindfulness practice does have solid evidence behind it). It's about systematically rebuilding your ability to focus and think deeply.

Start small - set aside just 15 minutes a day for completely focused single-task work. No phone, no email, no distractions. Just you and whatever you're working on. It'll feel uncomfortable at first - maybe even impossible. But stick with it. Gradually increase the duration. Pay attention to what distracts you and systematically eliminates those distractions.

This brings us to continuous learning techniques - strategies for not just maintaining but actively expanding your cognitive capabilities. And here's where things get really interesting because the science of learning has advanced dramatically in recent years.

First principle: active recall beats passive review every time. Don't just read or highlight - test yourself. The act of retrieving information strengthens the neural pathways associated with that knowledge. This is why flashcards are so effective - they force you to actively recall information rather than just recognize it.

Second principle: spaced repetition is your friend. Don't cram - space out you're learning over time. This isn't just about convenience - it actually leads to better long-term retention. The optimal spacing depends on what you're learning, but generally, reviewing material just as you're starting to forget it is the sweet spot.

Third principle: interleaving beats blocking. Instead of practicing one thing over and over (blocking), mix up different but related topics or skills (interleaving). It feels harder in the moment, but it leads to better long-term learning and more flexible knowledge application.

But perhaps the most powerful learning technique is what I call "metacognitive practice" - actively thinking about and analyzing your own thinking and learning processes. This means regularly reflecting on what you're learning, how you're learning it, and what strategies are working best for you.

Global Cognitive Enhancement: Holistic Strategies for Human Potential

Redefining Personal and Collective Cognitive Development

Cognitive enhancement represents a multidimensional journey of human potential, transcending individual skill development to embrace a comprehensive approach to mental and emotional growth.

Global Cognitive Development Perspectives

Indigenous Cognitive Cultivation Practices

- Holistic mind-body-spirit integration
- Experiential learning methodologies
- Intergenerational wisdom transmission
- Ecological intelligence development

Key Principles:

- Cognitive skills embedded in cultural context
- Collective knowledge preservation
- Intuitive learning strategies
- Harmony with natural systems

Eastern Cognitive Enhancement Approaches

- Meditative cognitive training
- Mindfulness as cognitive development method
- Emotional intelligence cultivation
- Holistic personal development

Transformative Practices:

- Consciousness expansion techniques
- Integrated mental-physical training
- Subtle energy management
- Compassion as cognitive skill

Neuroplasticity and Cognitive Potential

Emerging Scientific Insights:

- Brain's lifelong learning capacity
- Emotional states as cognitive catalysts
- Neurological adaptation mechanisms
- Environmental influence on cognitive development
- Interconnected neural network plasticity

Technological Cognitive Enhancement

Innovative Development Vectors:

- Personalized cognitive training platforms
- Neurofeedback technologies
- Brain-computer interface development
- Adaptive learning algorithms
- Cognitive performance optimization tools

Psychological Dimensions of Learning

Holistic Development Frameworks:

- Emotional intelligence integration
- Trauma-informed learning approaches
- Psychological resilience cultivation
- Stress management as cognitive skill
- Narrative reconstruction techniques

Cross-Cultural Learning Strategies

Transformative Learning Principles:

- Context-responsive skill development
- Cultural intelligence cultivation
- Adaptive learning methodologies
- Collaborative knowledge creation
- Empathy as cognitive enhancement tool

Systemic Cognitive Development

Societal Transformation Potential:

- Education as lifelong process
- Community-based learning networks
- Intergenerational skill transmission
- Collective intelligence frameworks
- Adaptive social learning systems

Ethical Cognitive Enhancement Considerations

Critical Philosophical Domains:

- Nature of human potential
- Consciousness expansion
- Technological mediation of learning
- Equity in cognitive development
- Preservation of human agency

Holistic Wellness Integration

Comprehensive Development Approach:

- Physical health as cognitive foundation
- Nutritional cognitive support
- Movement and neural plasticity
- Sleep as cognitive regeneration
- Stress reduction as learning enabler

Emerging Research Frontiers

Cutting-Edge Exploration Areas:

- Epigenetic learning mechanisms
- Quantum consciousness research
- Neurological network mapping
- Emotional intelligence neuroscience
- Collective cognitive potential

Conclusion

Cognitive enhancement is not a destination, but a continuous, dynamic journey of human potential. It represents our species' most profound capacity - the ability to grow, adapt, and transform beyond our current limitations.

Our cognitive future lies in embracing complexity, cultivating compassion, and recognizing the infinite potential within each human mind.

Learning is not something we do - it is something we are, continuously becoming.

Keep a learning journal. Track what works and what doesn't. Experiment with different approaches. The goal isn't just to learn specific information or skills, but to become a more effective learner overall.

And here's where all these strategies come together - they're not just isolated interventions, but parts of an integrated system for cognitive enhancement. The exercise makes the sleep more effective, which makes the learning more efficient, which makes the focus training more productive, and so on.

The key is to start small and build gradually. Don't try to overhaul your entire life overnight. Pick one or two strategies that resonate with you and implement them consistently. Once they become habits, add another. Think of it as progressive overload for your brain - gradually increasing the cognitive demands in a sustainable way.

Remember, this isn't just about fighting cognitive decline - it's about actively enhancing your mental capabilities. The human brain is remarkably plastic, capable of growth and adaptation throughout life. But like any complex system, it needs the right inputs and environment to thrive.

The strategies I've outlined aren't magic bullets, but they are proven tools for cognitive enhancement. They require effort and consistency, yes, but the returns are more than worth it. We're talking about your mind here - the tool you use to perceive, understand, and interact with everything in your life.

Start today. Pick one strategy - maybe it's starting a regular exercise routine, or implementing a digital sunset, or beginning a daily focused work practice. Commit to it for thirty days. Track your progress. Notice the changes in how you think and feel.

Because here's the thing: while the Great Dimming might be a societal trend, your personal cognitive trajectory is still largely under your control. You have the power to protect and enhance your mental capabilities, to build a brain that's not just resistant to decline but primed for growth and development.

The tools are there. The science is solid. The rest is up to you.

Choose wisely. Your future self will thank you.

Chapter 12: The Road Ahead

Systemic Solutions and Future Implications

We've reached the home stretch. We've explored the problem from every angle, looked at individual solutions, and now it's time to think bigger. Much bigger. Because while personal interventions are important, they're not enough. The Great Dimming isn't just an individual problem - it's a systemic one, and it demands systemic solutions.

Let's start with the elephant in the room: education. Our current educational system was designed for an industrial age that no longer exists, yet we're still using it to prepare students for a future that's arriving faster than we can comprehend. It's like trying to teach spacecraft engineering using a manual for horse-drawn carriages.

The data is clear: traditional classroom models are becoming increasingly ineffective at developing the kind of cognitive capabilities we need in the modern world. Test scores are one thing, but the real crisis is in the development of critical thinking, creative problem-solving, and adaptive learning skills - precisely the abilities that will matter most in the coming decades.

I've been talking with a consortium of educators and neuroscientists on what we call the "Cognitive First" curriculum model. The basic premise is simple but revolutionary: instead of organizing education around subject matter, we organize it around cognitive skill development. Math isn't just about learning equations - it's about developing pattern recognition and logical reasoning. Literature isn't just about reading stories - it's about building narrative comprehension and emotional intelligence.

The preliminary results from pilot programs are promising. Schools that have implemented even partial versions of this approach are seeing significant improvements in both traditional academic metrics and measures of cognitive development. One particularly striking finding: students in these programs show a 40% smaller decline in fluid intelligence compared to their peers in traditional schools.

But curriculum redesign is just the beginning. We need to fundamentally rethink how we teach. The traditional model of passive information transfer - what Paulo Freire called the "banking model" of education - is quite literally working against how our brains actually learn and develop.

Instead, we need to move toward what I call "cognitive apprenticeship" - a model that combines direct skill development with practical application and metacognitive training. This means less lecturing and more doing, less memorization and more problem-solving, less testing and more real-world application.

One fascinating example comes from a high school in Finland that's been experimenting with this approach. They've eliminated traditional subject boundaries and instead organize learning around real-world problems and projects. Students might spend six weeks working on a community environmental project that integrates biology, chemistry, math, and civic education - all while developing crucial cognitive skills like systems thinking and collaborative problem-solving.

But education reform, crucial as it is, is just one piece of the puzzle. We need to talk about environmental protection measures because the evidence linking environmental toxins to cognitive decline is becoming impossible to ignore

Here's a sobering statistic: every 10-point increase in air pollution levels is associated with a cognitive decline equivalent to aging two additional years. That's right - breathing dirty air quite literally ages your brain. And yet, our current environmental protection measures are woefully inadequate to address this threat.

We need comprehensive legislation that recognizes cognitive health as a crucial environmental concern. This means stricter regulations on neurotoxic chemicals, better monitoring of air and water quality, and aggressive action on climate change (which, by the way, is itself associated with declining cognitive function through multiple pathways).

But environmental protection isn't just about regulation - it's about redesigning our cities and communities to support cognitive health. Green spaces, for instance, aren't just nice to look at - they're associated with better cognitive development in children and slower cognitive decline in adults. Access to nature should be considered a public health necessity, not a luxury.

Speaking of public health, let's talk about early intervention programs. The science is clear: the earlier we intervene to support cognitive development, the better the outcomes. Yet, our current approach to early childhood development is a patchwork of underfunded programs and missed opportunities.

We need universal access to high-quality early childhood education, regular cognitive health screenings, and support services for families. The return on investment for these programs is astronomical - every dollar spent on early intervention saves society between seven and twelve dollars in future costs.

But early intervention isn't enough. We need robust community support systems that promote cognitive health throughout the lifespan. This means everything from public libraries and community education programs to senior centers that offer cognitive enrichment activities.

One particularly promising model comes from Japan, where "brain training" centers for older adults have become as common as fitness centers. These facilities offer structured cognitive exercise programs, social interaction, and ongoing monitoring of cognitive health. The results? Participants show significantly slower rates of cognitive decline compared to their peers.

Now, let's talk about the workplace because that's where most adults spend the majority of their waking hours. The current model of knowledge work - with its endless meetings, constant interruptions, and chronic stress - is basically designed to degrade cognitive function.

We need workplace cognitive support programs that go beyond the occasional wellness seminar. This means redesigning work environments to support focused attention, implementing "cognitive ergonomics" standards (just like we have physical ergonomics standards), and creating cultures that value mental recovery as much as productivity.

Some forward-thinking companies are already moving in this direction. One tech firm I talked to has implemented what they call "deep work windows" - four-hour blocks where all meetings and internal communications are banned, allowing employees to focus on complex cognitive tasks without interruption. The result? A 30% increase in both productivity and employee satisfaction.

But perhaps the most crucial systemic change we need involves technology use guidelines. We can't put the digital genie back in the bottle, but we can be much more intentional about how we integrate technology into our lives and institutions.

Global Technological and Societal Transformation: A Comprehensive Analysis

Reimagining Human Connection in the Digital Age

The intersection of technology, society, and human cognition represents a complex, dynamic landscape of unprecedented change, challenging traditional understanding of social interaction, communication, and collective intelligence.

Emerging Societal Paradigms

1. Digital Tribalism and Identity Formation
- Radical transformation of social belonging
- Online communities as primary social networks
- Geographically dispersed but culturally integrated groups
- Identity construction through digital personas
1. Cognitive Adaptation Mechanisms
- Neurological rewiring in response to technological environments
- Reduced linear thinking capabilities

- Enhanced parallel processing and information integration
- Shifted attention management strategies

Cross-Cultural Technology Impact

Global Observations:

- Varying technological integration rates
- Cultural differences in digital interaction
- Uneven cognitive adaptation processes
- Technological colonialism and knowledge dissemination

Psychological Transformation Vectors

Key Psychological Shifts:

- Reduced face-to-face interaction skills
- Enhanced digital communication competencies
- Altered emotional processing mechanisms
- Fragmented attention and multitasking tendencies
- Increased social anxiety in physical interactions

Technological Mediation of Human Experience

Critical Analysis Dimensions:

- Algorithmic curation of personal experiences
- Reduced spontaneity in social interactions
- Artificial intelligence as social intermediary

- Emotional regulation through digital interfaces
- Privacy and identity complexity

Neurological Adaptation Insights

Emerging Research Reveals:

- Brain plasticity in response to digital environments
- Reduced deep processing capabilities
- Enhanced rapid information scanning skills
- Modified memory storage and retrieval mechanisms
- Altered dopamine response systems

Social Communication Evolution

Communication Transformation Characteristics:

- Visual and emoji-based language development
- Reduced verbal complexity
- Increased global linguistic hybridization
- Real-time translation technologies
- Contextual communication compression

Systemic Innovation Potential

Transformative Strategies:

- Develop digital literacy frameworks
- Create intentional disconnection protocols

- Design human-centered technological interfaces
- Promote cross-cultural digital understanding
- Develop adaptive cognitive support systems

Technological Ethics and Governance

Emerging Governance Models:

- Algorithmic accountability mechanisms
- Human rights in digital spaces
- Cognitive autonomy protection
- Technological impact assessment frameworks
- Ethical AI development guidelines

Global Inequality Considerations

Critical Systemic Challenges:

- Digital divide perpetuating social stratification
- Unequal technological access
- Knowledge monopolization
- Cognitive capability disparities
- Cultural homogenization risks

Philosophical and Existential Implications

Fundamental Questions Emerging:

- Definition of human consciousness

- Boundaries between human and technological intelligence
- Nature of social connection
- Individual agency in algorithmic environments
- Meaning of human experience

Conclusion

The digital transformation represents more than technological change - it's a profound reimagining of human potential, social interaction, and collective intelligence.

Our challenge lies not in resisting change, but in consciously shaping technological evolution to enhance, rather than diminish, our fundamental human capacities.

The future of humanity will be defined by our ability to navigate this complex, dynamic technological landscape with wisdom, empathy, and intentional creativity.

We need evidence-based guidelines for technology use in schools, workplaces, and public spaces. This isn't about limiting access - it's about optimizing it for cognitive health. For instance, research shows that certain types of screen activity are much more detrimental to cognitive development than others. Yet, our current approach to "screen time" treats all digital activity as equivalent.

Now, let's peer into the future and consider where all this might be heading. Based on current trends and modeling, we're looking at three possible scenarios for cognitive evolution in the coming decades.

The "Business as Usual" scenario is grim. If we continue on our current trajectory, we're looking at a 15-20% decline in average cognitive capability over the next generation. This isn't just about IQ scores - it's about our collective ability to solve problems, think creatively, and adapt to new challenges.

The economic implications are staggering. Our models suggest that unchecked cognitive decline could reduce global GDP by up to 10% by 2050, primarily through decreased innovation, lower productivity, and increased healthcare costs. This doesn't even account for the indirect effects on social cohesion, democratic functioning, and cultural development.

But there's also an "Intervention" scenario, where we implement the kind of systemic solutions we've been discussing. In this model, we could not only halt the decline but potentially reverse it. The key is early action - our models suggest that the effectiveness of interventions decreases dramatically if we wait more than 5–10 years to implement them.

The most interesting (and perhaps most likely) is what I call the "Adaptation" scenario. In this future, human cognition doesn't so much decline as transform. We develop new cognitive capabilities while losing others, creating a fundamentally different kind of intelligence than what we've traditionally valued and measured.

Global Cognitive Evolution: Reimagining Human Potential

Transcending Traditional Paradigms of Intelligence

Human cognitive potential represents a dynamic, multidimensional ecosystem of adaptation, creativity, and transformative capacity that extends far beyond traditional measurement frameworks.

Global Cognitive Transformation Perspectives

1. Indigenous Wisdom Paradigms
- Holistic intelligence conceptualization
- Ecological cognition integration
- Collective knowledge systems
- Intuitive problem-solving approaches

Transformative Principles:

- Intelligence as relational capacity
- Interconnectedness as cognitive foundation
- Wisdom beyond individual computation
- Sustainability as cognitive framework
1. Emerging Global Cognitive Models
- Collaborative intelligence networks
- Transdisciplinary thinking approaches
- Cultural cognitive diversity
- Adaptive learning ecosystems

Key Characteristics:

- Beyond individual cognitive capabilities
- Collective problem-solving intelligence
- Fluid knowledge integration
- Contextual intelligence development

Technological Cognitive Symbiosis

Emerging Developmental Trajectories:

- Human-artificial intelligence collaboration
- Cognitive enhancement technologies
- Neurological interface innovations
- Adaptive learning platforms
- Distributed intelligence networks

Philosophical Dimensions of Cognitive Evolution

Fundamental Transformation Vectors:

- Redefinition of human consciousness
- Expanded understanding of intelligence
- Cognitive capabilities beyond current limitations
- Interconnected global intelligence systems
- Ethical considerations of cognitive enhancement

Systemic Cognitive Development

Societal Transformation Potential:

- Education as continuous adaptation
- Global knowledge exchange platforms
- Intergenerational learning networks
- Collective intelligence frameworks
- Adaptive social learning mechanisms

Ethical and Philosophical Considerations

Critical Inquiry Domains:

- Nature of human potential
- Consciousness expansion boundaries
- Technological mediation of intelligence
- Preservation of human agency
- Equity in cognitive development

Emerging Research Frontiers

Cutting-Edge Exploration Areas:

- Quantum consciousness research
- Neuroplasticity mechanisms
- Epigenetic learning potential
- Collective cognitive networks
- Transformative learning methodologies

Cultural Intelligence Frameworks

Comprehensive Development Approaches:

- Multicultural cognitive integration
- Empathy as cognitive capability
- Contextual intelligence development
- Cross-cultural knowledge synthesis
- Adaptive communication strategies

Technological Cognitive Innovation

Transformative Technologies:

- Brain-computer interfaces
- Neurological optimization platforms
- Adaptive learning algorithms
- Personalized cognitive enhancement tools
- Global intelligence network development

Holistic Wellness Integration

Comprehensive Development Principles:

- Mind-body-spirit cognitive approach
- Emotional intelligence cultivation
- Neurological resilience strategies
- Stress management as cognitive skill
- Integrated wellness frameworks

Conclusion

Cognitive evolution represents humanity's most profound journey of self-discovery and transformation. We are not passive recipients of intelligence, but active creators of expanding consciousness.

Our future lies not in preserving existing cognitive structures, but in embracing our capacity for continuous adaptation, creativity, and collective understanding.

Intelligence is not a fixed state, but a dynamic, evolving expression of human potential.

This brings us to cultural implications, which are perhaps the most fascinating aspect of all this. The way we think shapes everything from our art and entertainment to our social structures and value systems. A shift in cognitive capabilities isn't just a medical or educational issue - it's a transformation of human culture itself.

We're already seeing early signs of this in changing patterns of cultural consumption and creation. The rise of short-form video content, the decline of long-form reading, the emergence of new forms of digital art and expression - these aren't just technological changes, they're manifestations of shifting cognitive patterns.

But here's where it gets really interesting: our ability to implement effective interventions might itself be compromised by cognitive decline. It's a bit like trying to repair a boat while you're sailing in it - and the boat is also your repair tool.

This is why timing is so crucial. The window for implementing effective systemic solutions might be shorter than we think. As cognitive decline progresses, our collective capacity to understand and address the problem could diminish, creating a kind of cognitive catch-22.

What is the bottom line? The future isn't written yet, but the pen is definitely in our hands. The systemic solutions we've discussed - from educational reform to environmental protection to workplace redesign - are all feasible. We have the knowledge, the technology, and the resources to implement them.

What we need now is the wisdom to recognize the urgency of the situation and the will to act on it. This isn't just about preserving cognitive capabilities - it's about actively shaping the future of human intelligence.

The next few years will be crucial. The decisions we make about education, environment, public health, and technology will have cascading effects on cognitive development for generations to come. We need to think systemically, act decisively, and move quickly.

But here's the hopeful part: unlike many global challenges, this one comes with a clear roadmap for solution. We know what works. We have evidence-based interventions at both the individual and systemic level. We can measure progress and adjust course as needed.

The question isn't whether we can address the Great Dimming - it's whether we will choose to do so. And that choice needs to be made soon, while we still have the collective cognitive capabilities to implement complex, systemic solutions.

This is our moment. The future of human intelligence - and by extension, human civilization - hangs in the balance. The solutions are there. The science is clear. The tools are available.

All that remains is for us to act.

The choice, as they say, is ours. Let's hope we're still smart enough to make the right one.

Conclusion: Rekindling Our Cognitive Fire

As we reach the end of our journey through the complex landscape of the Great Dimming, it's time to take stock of where we stand and chart a course forward. The evidence we've explored paints a picture that is both sobering and hopeful - sobering in the scope and scale of the cognitive challenges we face, but hopeful in the glimmers of solutions and success stories that light the way ahead.

Let's recap the key insights that have emerged from our exploration:

The decline in cognitive capabilities is real, widespread, and accelerating. From falling IQ scores and diminished problem-solving abilities to weakened memory and attention, the data points to a slow but steady erosion of our mental faculties across a wide range of measures. This dimming of our collective intelligence isn't just an academic curiosity - it has profound implications for our ability to navigate the complex challenges of the 21st century.

The causes are multifaceted and interwoven. There is no single smoking gun, no lone culprit to blame. Instead, what we're seeing is the convergence of multiple factors - environmental toxins, lifestyle changes, educational shortcomings, technological disruptions, and societal shifts - all interacting in complex ways to reshape our cognitive environment. Addressing this challenge will require a systems-level approach that recognizes these interconnections.

Yet within this complexity lies cause for optimism. Across a wide range of contexts - from schools and communities pioneering new approaches to cognitive health, to individuals adopting evidence-based practices for mental enhancement - we're seeing proof that positive change is possible. These bright spots demonstrate that the trajectory of intelligence isn't fixed - that with the right interventions and innovations, we can not only stem the tide of decline but potentially unleash new waves of cognitive flourishing.

Ok now, where do we go from here? How do we translate these insights into a roadmap for individual and collective action?

At the personal level, the path is increasingly clear. A growing body of research has identified a core set of lifestyle practices - regular exercise, quality sleep, healthy nutrition, focused attention, continuous learning - that can significantly protect and enhance cognitive function at any age. By adopting these practices and making them a priority, each of us has the power to take control of our own cognitive destiny.

But as powerful as individual action can be, it's not enough on its own. Because the forces shaping our cognitive environment operate at a societal level, they demand societal-level responses. This is where the real work - and the real opportunity - lies.

It starts with a fundamental shift in how we think about cognitive health - not as a private good or personal indulgence, but as a public necessity, as vital to the functioning of our communities and institutions as clean air or safe streets. Just as we've come to recognize the importance of environmental protection and public health, we need to elevate cognitive well-being to a similar level of collective concern and investment.

What might this look like in practice? The examples we've seen from forward-thinking communities around the world provide a template. By redesigning public spaces to integrate cognitive stimulation, creating intergenerational learning opportunities, developing neighborhood-based brain health resources, and implementing comprehensive environmental and education strategies, these communities are demonstrating what's possible when cognitive health becomes a shared civic priority.

At the policy level, we need to match this local innovation with bold systemic reforms. This means enacting robust environmental protections to safeguard our brains from neurotoxic pollutants. It means reimagining education, not just to impart knowledge but to cultivate the core cognitive capabilities - creativity, critical thinking, mental flexibility - that will define success in the coming century. It means elevating brain science and cognitive research to a national priority, on par with the moonshot initiatives that have driven other great leaps forward. And it means regulating technology - particularly as it relates to children and youth - to ensure that our digital tools are designed to enhance rather than erode our cognitive capacities.

None of this will be easy. The challenges are complex, the inertia is formidable, and the stakes could not be higher. But if there is one thing that the story of human progress has taught us, it's that we are at our best when we're pushing the boundaries of what's possible - when we're using our intelligence to illuminate new frontiers, to solve problems that once seemed intractable, to imagine and create better versions of ourselves and our world.

In many ways, the Great Dimming represents the ultimate frontier - the landscape of the mind itself, the terrain of human cognition in all its infinite potential and vulnerability. To navigate this frontier successfully will require all of our ingenuity and resolve. It will require us to question long-held assumptions, to overturn entrenched paradigms, to reimagine the very foundations of how we live, work, learn and grow.

But if we can rise to this challenge - if we can muster the collective will and wisdom to place the cultivation of our cognitive capital at the center of our societal agenda - then I believe we can not only turn the tide of the Great Dimming, but open up vistas of human possibility that we can barely imagine today.

Imagine a world where every child is born into an environment optimized to nurture their unique cognitive gifts - where the concept of "learning loss" becomes a relic of the past, replaced by an educational paradigm that unlocks the full spectrum of human intelligences.

Imagine a world where our cities and communities are designed, from the ground up, as landscapes for lifelong cognitive enhancement - where every public space is an invitation to explore, to create, to stretch the boundaries of what our minds can do.

Imagine a world where technological progress is guided, first and foremost, by the imperative to expand rather than contract the frontiers of human thought - where our digital tools evolve in symbiosis with the boundless possibilities of the human brain.

Imagine a world where the pursuit of knowledge, the joy of deep understanding, the thrill of the mental challenge well-met, are not just the province of a cognitive elite, but the birthright of every human being - where the flame of genius burns bright in every heart, and the light of reason illuminates every mind.

This is the world that the science of cognitive enhancement invites us to create. A world where the trajectory of intelligence bends ever upward, where the capabilities of the human mind expand in lockstep with the complexities of the challenges we face. A world where the Great Dimming becomes a distant memory, replaced by an enduring commitment to the nurturance and unleashing of humanity's greatest gift: the miracle of our cognition.

Is this a utopian vision? Perhaps. But it is a vision rooted in the evidence of what is possible - in the extraordinary scientific revelations of neuroplasticity and cognitive reserve, in the pioneering educational models that are unleashing new dimensions of human potential, in the quiet everyday triumphs of individuals and communities who are finding new ways to kindle the spark of intelligence against all odds.

Most of all, it is a vision that recognizes that the fate of our cognitive future is not preordained - that the choices we make today, as individuals and as a society, will shape the minds and therefore the possibilities of generations to come.

As we stand at this pivotal juncture in the human story, let us seize that responsibility with all the courage and commitment it demands. Let us dare to place the cultivation of our collective cognition at the very heart of our shared ambitions. Let us reimagine our schools and cities, our policies and priorities, our technologies, and cultural touchstones, in the light of this overarching imperative. Let us kindle a new Renaissance of the Mind - a great global awakening of our intellectual and creative energies, in service to a brighter cognitive future for all.

The journey ahead will not be easy. It will require us to confront uncomfortable truths, to overturn entrenched paradigms, to venture into uncharted territories of thought and action. But if there is one thing that the long arc of human history teaches us, it is that we are at our best when we are reaching for the highest within ourselves and each other - when we are using the gift of our intelligence to push back the boundaries of the possible and to weave new realities out of the raw materials of our dreams.

We begin that work today, you and I, in whatever sphere of influence we command. Whether as educators or entrepreneurs, parents or policymakers, researchers, or citizens, let us bring the lens of cognitive enhancement to bear on all our endeavors. Let us ask ourselves, at every juncture: how can we design our lives, our organizations, our society itself, to more fully sustain and unleash the mighty force of human cognition? How can we create a world that does not dim but ignites the spark of intelligence in every mind, that kindles the flame of knowledge and creativity and critical insight as the very lifeblood of our civilization?

The answers to these questions will not come all at once. But if we hold fast to the vision, and stay true to the evidence, I have no doubt that they will come.

And when they do - when we have built a world that truly nurtures human cognition in all its wondrous diversity and untapped potential - we will look back on the Great Dimming not as an inevitable decline, but as the crucible that forged our commitment to a brighter cognitive future. We will see it as the darkness before a great dawn - the prelude to a new era of enlightenment and intellectual flourishing that will make all the struggles and setbacks worthwhile.

This is the promise and the possibility that lies before us. It will not be easy to achieve - nothing worth having ever is. But I believe with all my heart that it is a promise worth fighting for - and that we are the ones, each in our own way, who were born to fight for it.

The future of the human mind, in all its infinite potential, is in our hands. Let us rise to this great calling of our time. Let us rekindle the light of reason, reignite the sparks of curiosity and creativity, and blaze a trail to a brighter cognitive tomorrow.

Together, let us dispel the Great Dimming - and unleash the radiant dawn of a new Age of Cognition.

Research Citations Analysis

Verified Studies on IQ Decline:

Bratsberg, B., & Rogeberg, O. (2018). The Flynn effect and its reversal are both environmentally caused. Proceedings of the National Academy of Sciences, 115(26), 6674-6678.

This is a real study from the Ragnar Frisch Centre for Economic Research in Norway

Analyzed IQ scores from Norwegian military conscripts between 1970-2009

Found a decline of 2.5 IQ points per decade

Dutton, E., van der Linden, D., & Lynn, R. (2016). The negative Flynn Effect: A systematic literature review. Intelligence, 59, 163-169.

Documents IQ declines in several developed countries

Provides meta-analysis of multiple studies showing reversal of the Flynn effect

Woodley of Menie, M. A., et al. (2018). Communicating intelligence research: Media misrepresentation, the Gould Effect, and unexpected forces. Intelligence, 70, 80-87.

Reviews evidence for declining cognitive ability across multiple measures